THE PRISTINE ROCKIES

THE PRISTINE ROCKIES

117 FULL COLOUR PHOTOGRAPHS

TEXT AND PHOTOGRAPHS BY
GEORGE BRYBYCIN

GB PUBLISHING

We have choices, we make choices

What suits us better: big stumps or big, healthy, beautiful trees? Since one hectare of forest produces 6 tons of pure oxygen and one large tree absorbs and neutralize 5 kg of carbon monoxide a year, what should our choice be?

Should we clear cut all of our forests and breathe only carbon monoxide and dioxide or limit tree cutting instead, plant millions of new trees, breathe pure oxygen and stay perfectly healthy?

If we would learn to use timber products, especially paper, more wisely, that would help save 40 % of trees cut.

If we would enact the law: for every tree cut, four new trees must be planted and each city property must have 40% of its area devoted to trees, perhaps then we could sleep well and have green dreams about our bright and healthy future.
A rational choice.

With this humble creation
George Brybycin
celebrates a little milestone:
his 30th publication

Introduction

Those who are familiar with the work of the prolific George Brybycin will immediately notice that the photo selection in this volume is quite different from his previous publications. This volume features the gentler, softer, more colourful aspects of the Rockies. There are fewer photos of the starker beauty of high altitude landscapes and more meadows, flowers, lakes and rivers.

The word pristine is derived from the Latin pristinus - which means original; former; belonging to the earliest time. Nature that is not affected by time or human interference, is unspoiled, wild and pristine.

The Canadian Rockies, at least those areas which are part of National and Provincial Parks - or in the far north, precisely fit this description and are the focus of this volume. On the other hand, at a time when the world's ecology is very ill and on a sharp decline, perhaps using the word pristine at present, is stretching reality a bit.

In the southern Rockies, there is little population: a few resort areas, serving tourists, do exist but have no real impact on the local ecology. In the northern parts, a permanent population almost does not exist - except for a few small service centers along the roads: gas stations, motels and a very few native settlements, and the large pristine wilderness does exist.

However, mining, logging and the oil industry - a great concern, negatively affect some areas because these activities leave long-lasting, or even permanent scars on the fragile mountain environment. As an example, consider the far north, where it takes over 200 years for a tree to grow to maturity. When the topsoil is removed by strip mining, it may take up to 80 years for vegetation to grow back.

The right balance between development and conservation must be found, especially in mountainous regions, because mountains are weather makers and air purifiers, as well as a source of drinking water for man and beast. It would be wonderful if we could declare the entire Canadian Rocky Mountains as a National Park. It may soon be a necessity, as other green areas may soon be gone, and we will still need fresh air to breathe and pure water to drink.

Instead of open pit mining, which ruins the local ecology, we should maintain a large wildlife population and rich flora in order to bring ecotourism to the north in a big way. This way we get the same financial benefits without ruining the environment.

The southern Rockies' most attractive areas are well protected by their National Park status and remain more or less wild and pristine.

This volume features splendid scenery from Banff, Jasper, Kootenay, Yoho and Waterton National Parks as well as a few Provincial Parks. The flora and fauna here is always gorgeous and plentiful, but one may not see it along the highways since some roads are now fenced off to prevent wildlife deaths caused by speeding automobiles.

So take a short hike up into the mountain meadows and you will see a true paradise - for nature's best showcase, visit between mid-July and mid-August.

In recent years, Black and Grizzly Bears seem to be plentiful and conflicts between them and humans are on the rise – most likely because of our encroachment on their home territories. Quite a few deaths and serious injuries have occurred, so caution and a knowledge of current conditions would be advisable before heading into the woods.

This volume is intended to show pristine areas only; they might be by the roadside, next to a small resort town or thirty kilometers into the wilderness. One will find no hotels, buses or power lines here. After all, this, George Brybycin's 30th book, is entitled "The Pristine Rockies".

Enjoy it while it is here in all its wild and pristine beauty.

A Beautiful Journey

I have been to the Tonquin Valley, in Jasper National Park, many times - including once in winter. Most of the photos I took there were on film stock that is unacceptable by today's production standards. Thus, I decided to return on a gorgeous September's day to recapture the area's stunning beauty on film.

When I arrived in Jasper, Park employees told me that there were no visitors at the moment and that I should watch out for the Grizzly Bears that frequent the area. I was really delighted when I happened upon a big, friendly fellow who was going my way - I figured two guys could certainly handle a Grizzly. Unfortunately, this fellow was so heavily laden with gear that the going was too slow for me. Since he was going to the Amethyst Lakes and I was off to climb Mt. Clitheroe (2747m), which was at least five kilometers further along, my new friend urged me to leave him and pick up my pace.

Since I broke my arm, I had not done many big trips and was in poor condition. The trip was about 26 km, so I hurried and made it to the slopes of Mt. Clitheroe. Since this was my first time on this mountain, little did I realize what trouble I was getting myself into.

Mt. Clitheroe is steep and covered with large boulders all the way to the top and there was no semi-flat area to set up my bivouac. Often, I could make a bit of ground flatter, but here, with all the boulders, there was nothing I could do. I could continue on to the summit in the dark, but who knew what obstacles might lie ahead. Besides, in such a situation, where one boulder may rest on another, one false move could trigger an avalanche of rock.

Then, I noticed a small patch of white on the west ridge. I climbed down to it and found, under the snow, solid ice. The patch was slanted steeply and ended in a 100m cliff. Since I had no other option, I took a sharp rock and pummeled the ice until I had a small, flat shelf. I secured it by surrounding it with large rocks, which promptly froze into the ice. Now, being certain that no packrats or bears would disturb me, I hit the sack.

Soon afterward, I noticed a bright shining through my bivouac canvas. When I looked out, I saw a great rainbow-like arch of colour adorning the northern horizon.

Being a total lover of the Northern Lights, I watched the shimmering spectacle and waiting for more developments. After another hour or so, it began to develop into the real thing. I jumped out of my bivouac and set my camera on a tripod. Unfortunately in about half the time of the exposure, it all but disappeared.

At the end of September, the cold, northwest wind is biting, so I crawled back into my sleeping bag. I realized that I was dehydrated and cold enough that I might not be able to sleep. The rest of the night turned out to be peaceful - though very cold.

At sunrise, I photographed The Ramparts and surrounding mountains from where I was and then, a half-hour later; I reached Mt. Clitheroe's summit. It was a cloudless, sunny day and made my exploration of the summit quite enjoyable. I found a number of flat places that can be used for bivouacking the next time I am here.

Mt. Clitheroe is not a high mountain, but provides a range of very interesting views: to the northeast is the Trident Range, dominated by Vertex Peak and Maccarib Pass in front of it; to the southeast stands Mt. Edith Cavell, silent and clad in solid white; to the right are jagged, Old Horn Mountain, massive Throne Mountain, the imposing Blackhorn Peak with Chevron Mountain behind it; to the south stand Thunderbolt Peak, Eremite Mountain and the lofty Mt. Erebus, which provides the emerald waters for Chrome Lake; to the southwest stands Mt. Fraser with its three peaks and then the incredibly rugged, glaciated The Ramparts, with its nine major peaks, continuing towards the west ending at Moat Pass and Lake. It is an incredible paradise to be sure.

Retrospectively, when I was coming up the trail, I met three young lads wearing light boots, T-shirts, jeans and not much more. "We are going to try Mt. Edith Cavell," they said. Since it was almost noon, I gently persuaded them that it might be too late in the day for them to attempt such a big mountain. So instead, they rushed up to the Tonquin Valley to look around.

As I approached Amethyst Lake, I encountered two of the three. When I asked where the third fellow was, they told me that he was a triathlete and had decided to run to the Maccarib Pass and down along Portal Creek to the road - about a 40 km run. The time was about 5 p.m. and that area is a permanent home to Grizzly Bears - injuries and fatal accidents are not uncommon there. This was the three's first time in the area and they were completely unaware of the dangers in the mountains.

Imagine what could happen if you took a wrong turn and wound up on a game trail that led nowhere; or if you sprained an ankle or broke a leg on a slippery, muddy path. Worse, what if you have encountered an aggressive Grizzly Bear while you were alone and 20 km deep in the wilderness?

When one gets lost in the wilderness in the late fall, while dressed for summer; one will most likely die when the nighttime temperature drops to -10°C. I will say again: never, ever separate - always stay with the group. In case of emergencies, you should always carry enough warm clothing and food to survive for an extra day or two. No one is invincible, not even you.

Exploring the charm and majesty of the mountains can be challenging, enriching and enjoyable, but make sure you know your limits. Know when to turn back so that you can return alive and in one piece, so that you may enjoy many more beautiful journeys.

Mount Robson Magic

The very first time I laid eyes on the legendary monarch of the Canadian Rockies - Mount Robson (3954m), many, many moons ago in eastern British Columbia; I was overwhelmed by the desire to set foot on its mighty, ice-capped summit. A personal obsession, an oromania as the Greeks call mountain madness, was born that day.

Through serious research, I found out that many try to climb Mt. Robson every year, but rarely do they make it to the summit. Being a vigorous young fellow, and full of bravado and zest - not to mention naivete - I decided to do it... solo! An almost impossible task to be sure.

For the next fifteen years I stubbornly tried to make it, but year after year, the mighty mountain and its frightfully unpredictable weather found a way to defeat me - thwarting my daring with an arsenal of calamities. Thus, in time, my dashing "climb them all" attitude was replaced with a more mature wisdom. I realized that the task was inconceivable - definitely too much to ask of a single person and so I hesitantly abandoned the idea. Now, every year, I go to Mt. Robson to say hello to the undefeated mountain and take a hike to Kinney Lake, or backpack to Berg Lake and scramble up a few slopes in the valley - like most reasonable people.

One warm summer day, I decided to tackle the southwest slopes of Mt. Robson once again - just to scramble up above the timberline to get a photo of Kinney Lake that was not obscured by the trees. The day was splendid and I admired the scenery while getting ready to take some photographs - I was totally mesmerized by the ambience of my surroundings. Suddenly, I was rudely interrupted by a crack of thunder that ruined the magic and tranquility of the moment. Concerned, I looked to the west and saw scary looking black clouds moving rapidly toward me. I immediately realized that this was not one of nature's little jokes. The black clouds were moving at incredible speeds just above my head - accompanied by intense and frightening thunder and lightning. Such a williwaws storm put me in a very dangerous predicament on the exposed slope of the mountain, I thought. I quickly assessed the situation and, deciding to forget the photos, ran down the 45 degree slopes that were now drenched by rain - not yet aghast but knowing what could come next.

By the time I reached the forest, halfway down the slope, the wind and rain had reached calamitous proportions and near hurricane strength - causing large trees to come crashing down around me. "What to do," I thought. If I stay here, falling trees or deadly lightning might get me. So, genuinely scared, I ran willynilly - avoiding or jumping over freshly fallen trees. Frequently tumbling head over heels on the steep, wet slopes; covered to the ears in mud and somber as I could possibly get, I finally reached the bottom of that awesome mountain. I noticed that the flats by Kinney Lake were flooded to knee-deep level.

As often happens in the mountains, the storm passed as quickly as it had come and was soon gone - completely over.

As I walked down the trail, soggy, dirty and tired, I contemplated just how idiosyncratic the weather could be. It was good to be alive after such a brush with danger. It was a real hair-raising experience, I thought.

Farther down the trail, I watched the swollen, swift and muddy Robson River whipping fallen trees, bushes and debris away with incredible speed and power. Entire slopes had been wiped clean of trees and many were swept into the river by the downpour.

Suddenly, a very large tree trunk appeared in the muddy water, moving at great speed. The winding river could hardly keep the massive trunk afloat and, as it came to a sharp bend in the river, the tree could not negotiate the turn. I watched in amazement as the tree hit the rocky cliff and broke into five pieces as thought it was made of glass.

One may think that violence is a human specialty, but one would be wrong. Here, on this day, an incredible calamity came upon a peaceful paradise from out of nowhere - for no apparent reason - and caused so much damage. Why? One might think that nature would be peaceful, harmonious and fair. Perhaps this event was fair in nature's eyes? In a few years, these slopes will certainly become green with healthy new trees - and nature, wise and eternal, will turn through its cycle one more time.

In one day, that one small scramble on Mt. Robson taught me much more than any university could. The teacher, nature, had created many courses, which I sum up as: admire, discover, learn from nature but respect and even fear its unlimited might and power. What looks pleasant enough on a postcard can be extremely dangerous and even deadly in stormy weather.

Anyone who thinks too highly of himself, or feels invincible and important, should attempt to climb a mountain in stormy weather. There is nothing more humbling - and perhaps they would learn just how weak, little and vulnerable they are.

Leo – The Packrat

People who have been around the Rocky Mountains for awhile will remember the old Bow Hut, which used to be by the Wapta Icefield - it was an icebox, cold even in the summer.

Now it has been replaced by the new Bow Hut, which is located a bit lower and to the east where it is sheltered from the western winds behind moraine - and it is warmer, too. The new hut, however, lacks one thing that made the old hut special.

For many years, Leo the Packrat resided there; happily making a pretty good living the year round, courtesy of the many tourists - Packrat being the popular name for the Bushy-tailed Woodrat (Neotoma cinera).

The late autumn (November and December) was a lean time for Leo but he accumulated enough fat in the summer to get him through tough times. He never hibernated, but "entertained" mountain folks all year.

He lived under the old Bow Hut, but had two large holes to give him access whenever he wanted - especially at mealtime. With all due respect to Leo, he was an obnoxious fellow. He would join people while they were preparing or eating their meals and would unceremoniously grab a chunk of bread, cheese or sausage right out from under someone's nose! Then he would disappear to enjoy his feast.

As far as is known, Leo was a bachelor - living a solitary life and minding his own business. Some people really liked Leo, shared their food with him willingly and enjoyed his company. There were also those who did not like Leo - especially when he chewed holes in their backpacks or leather boots. Some, who were not aware of Leo's existence, would leave their food unprotected overnight and awaken to find that it was all messed up, chewed, or just eaten up.

Repeated attempts were made to beat up poor Leo, or chase him away but the quick and clever rat always dodged and escaped any assaults made on him. From his point of view, he had done nothing wrong. He was just trying to make a decent living in this cold and hostile place.

One day, Leo crossed the line. He stole a large bar of cheese from a climbing party. One climber executed a strong, quick swipe of an icesaw and chopped off Leo's head. Mixed feelings swept through the hut. Some were relieved by Leo's death; others were sad and some even cried.

A proper funeral was held the next morning and the long history of Leo the Rat came to an end.

While Leo, the bachelor lived alone, there are packrat families in many other locations.

Once upon a time, I scaled a small mountain (2800m) and bivouacked on the summit. Soon after I retired, something quite large rubbed against my shoulder. I chased it away but it returned almost immediately. By the dim light, I saw that it was unmistakably a packrat.

Knowing what these fellows are about, I got up and cached my food 20 meters from my shelter - covering it with large rocks. Later I heard some noises, but the rat never came back and I slept soundly.

The next morning, I shot several good photos and decided to have a nice breakfast. To my bewilderment, the rocks had been moved aside, there was a big hole in my food bag and the food (a very large sandwich, an apple, a banana and a bar of chocolate) was completely gone. All that remained was my water bottle. While sipping from the bottle, I spotted a big, fat packrat seated on a nearby rock - with a huge smile on its ugly, furry face as though to say "Thanks for the grub, guy." "You rat!" I said, though without anger or hatred and I headed off. Fortunately, my car was within a two-hour's travel and contained a good variety of food and drink.

In early summer, I went to photograph Bear Grass in Waterton Lakes National Park. From Cameron Lake, I took the Carthew Trail, photographing many flowers along the way. Since I had already climbed Mt. Carthew, I decided to climb, and bivouac on, Mt. Alderson. At an altitude of 2692m, the summit was still a bit snowy. From there, impressive vistas unfold in every direction and, being only 3 km north of the US border, I could see many majestic mountains north of the Logan Pass, as well as the lofty Mt. Cleveland - Alderson and Bertha Lakes were just below me.

I retired into my bivouac sack after sunset - tired by a long, hot day's hard work. A sudden movement along my shoulder woke me out of a sound sleep. I tried to squeeze whatever it was toward the bivouac wall, but it was too quick and escaped and ran away through the snow. In the moonlight, I recognized it as another packrat. Being familiar with the packrat's appetite and tenacity, I knew I wouldn't be getting much more sleep. I was tired and wanted to sleep, but the rat came back.

I decided to take my pepper spray for bears and teach the rodent a hard lesson. I didn't have to wait for long before the rat came back again and I fired a jet of pepper spray at him from a distance of about a meter. He ran away and I felt sad about inflicting such punishment on the poor guy - he just wanted to eat my food, like any other packrat.

Satisfied that the spray had worked, I laid back down to sleep. The peace lasted for less than a minute, and the rat was back! I was surprised, and thought that the spray hadn't worked properly, or was out-of-date. Since the rat was advancing toward me, without any hesitation or pity, I fired another jet of the spray. The rat retreated again, but I got quite a bit of spray over my face when the wind blew it back at me. Choking, and with watery eyes, I covered my face in my sleeping bag and survived. The spray *did* work. But soon, that tough little rat returned.

I had heard that these nasty guys were impossibly resilient and very persistent and now, I was learning about it first hand.

Leo had class and refinement - in the old Bow Hut, he rubbed shoulders with educated, upper class visitors. This rat displayed rough manners, even for a rat. So, reasoning that the rat would never give up and leave me alone, I got up, picked up my food bag and cached it some distance from my camp. Because of my previous experience, I used three layers of heavy, flat slabs which even I had trouble moving. The rat never bothered me again. He just wanted to supplement his diet with my fancy food. For awhile, I heard him working at my cache - trying to move away the rocks - but, being very tired, I fell asleep.

The next morning, I found the cache almost undisturbed. The large rock slabs were too heavy for the rat - I am happy that bears rarely frequent mountaintops.

The moral of the story is that if you bivouac below 3000m, you must securely cache your food or you won't get any sleep and a packrat will be very grateful!

*T*he Valley of the Ten Peaks. Banff National Park.

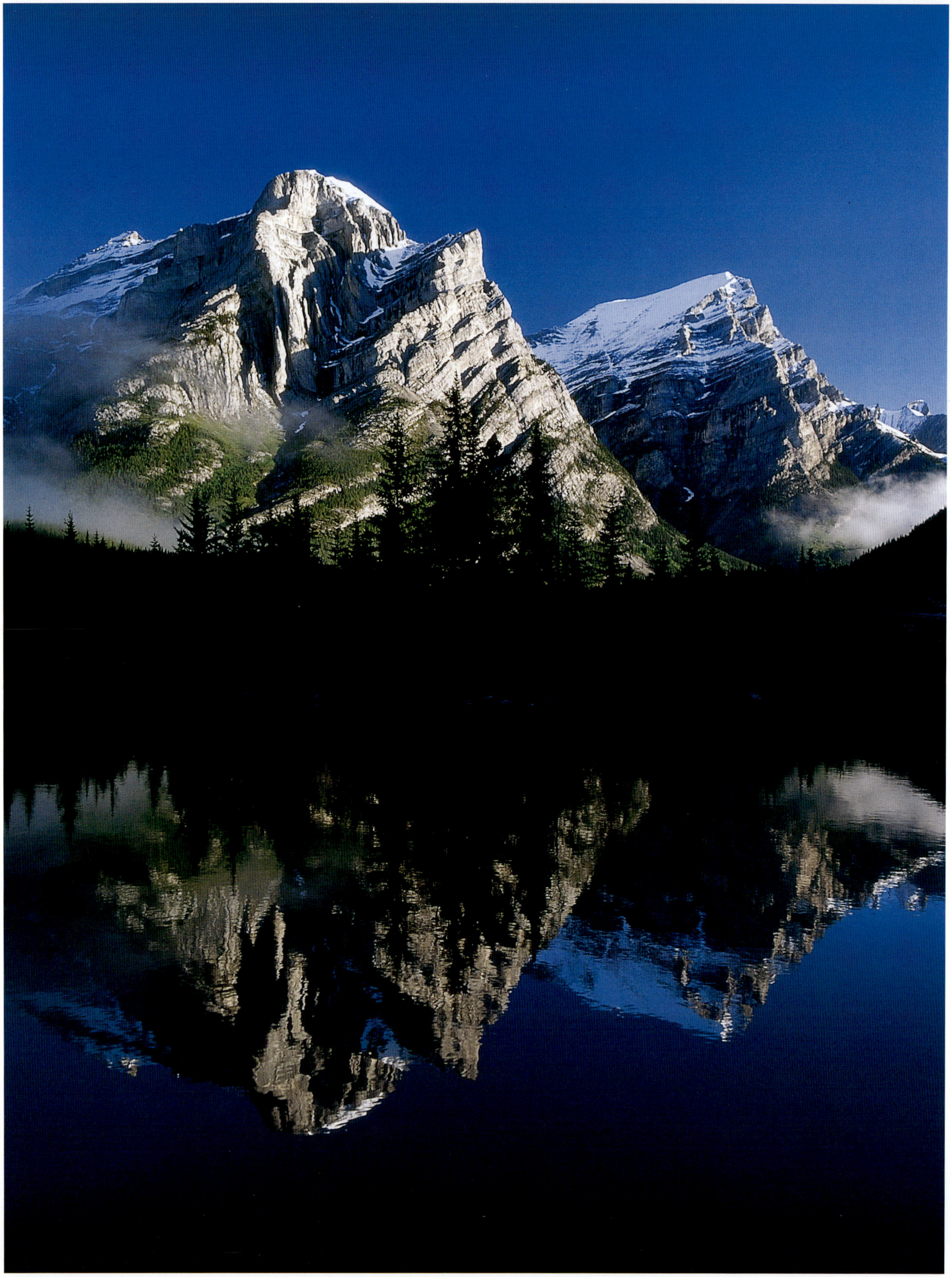

Pure, life-giving mountain water nourishes a small colony of Indian Paintbrushes, Fireweeds, herbs, grasses and trees. Wherever there is water, there is life. The Rockies are weather-makers, air and water purifiers, life givers.

Left: Mt. Kidd (2958m) - a massive, imposing two-peak mountain dominating the lower part of the Kananaskis Valley, reflected in a small tarn along the Kananaskis River. The lesser peak, on the left, stands at 2895m – though it appears to be higher.

A close-up look at the highest mountain in the Canadian Rockies, the monumental, snow and ice-capped Mt. Robson (3954m). The mountain's height creates its own climate. Moisture traveling from the Pacific crashes into the mountain, causing a generous amount of rain or snow. This is why the relatively dry Rockies have a rich, lush rainforest here.

The peaks of Mt. Rundle (2998m), not the highest, but still rugged and challenging, viewed from the north. Despite being located in a busy part of Banff National Park, the area still remains wild and beautiful. The mountain is named after missionary Robert T. Rundle, who first sighted it in 1847.

*I*n high mountains such as the Rockies, snow may fall at any time of the year. In the middle of August, snow fell at Bow Summit and these meadows were all white – by early afternoon it had all melted, except on the peaks, causing no damage to the hardy plants of the high meadows.

One of the showiest Rocky Mountain flowers, the Indian Paintbrush (Castilleja miniata) is endemic to the region and can be found over a wide range of altitudes. It prefers sunny, well - drained slopes and ledges. An associate plants of the Castilleja subspecies which are yellow, pink or rarely, white in colour and prefer a moister habitat.

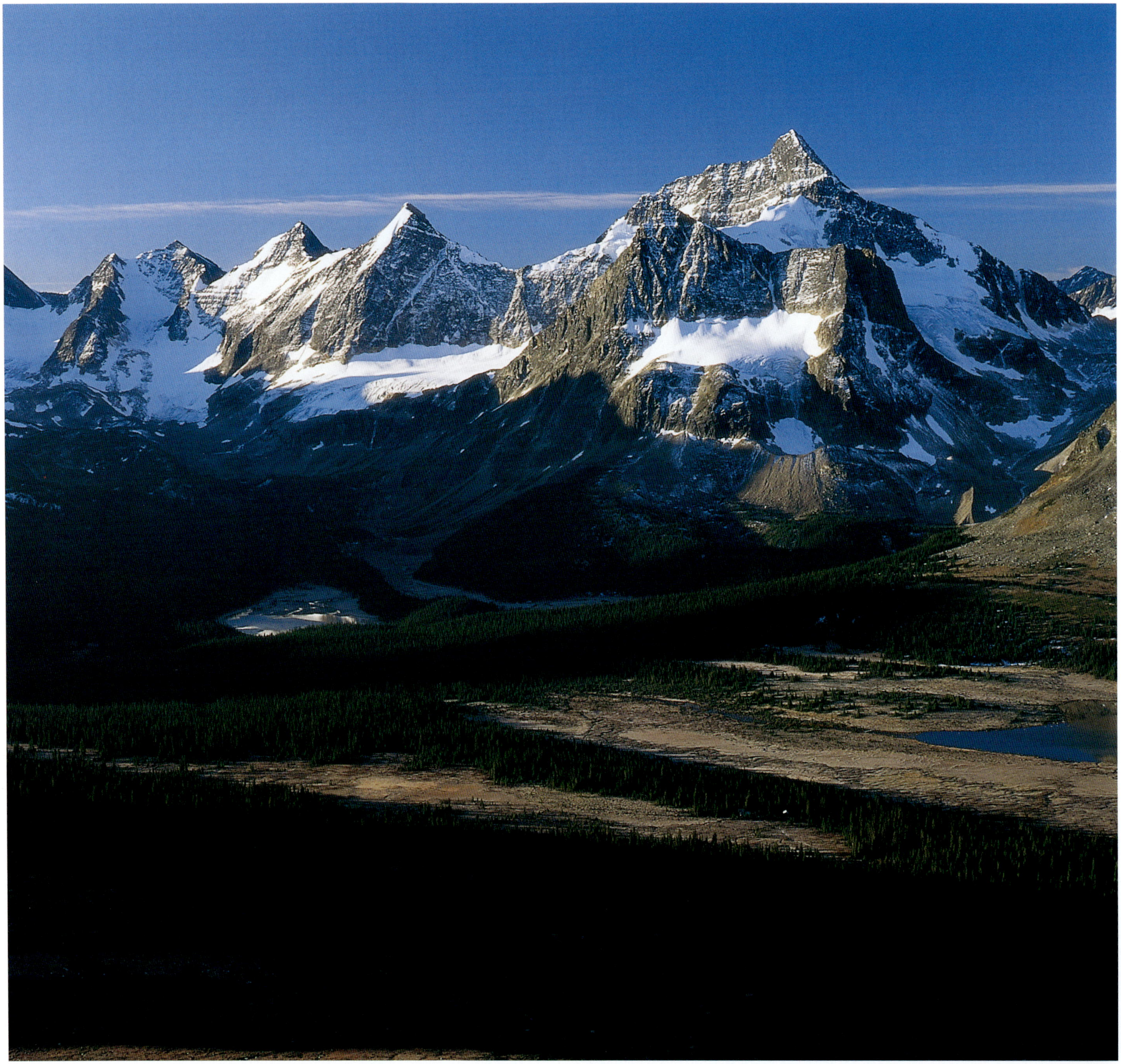

An icy desert, the Robson Glacier is one of the largest in the Rockies. It originates at Robson Cirque, high up between Mt. Robson and Mt. Resplendent, and is 8 km long. Global warming, pollution and other factors cause the glacier to melt about 15 m per year.

Left: *The Ramparts stretch for 15 km along the Amethyst Lakes, southwest of Tonquin Valley. Further to the south, the valley is lined by high, glaciated mountains like Eremite Mtn and its glacier, left. The lofty Mt. Erebus (3119m) dominates the scene – in front of it is the lesser Outpost Peak. The turquoise Chrome Lake is on the left and the south end of Amethyst Lake is on the right. This photo was taken from Mt. Clitheroe on a glorious September morning. Jasper National Park.*

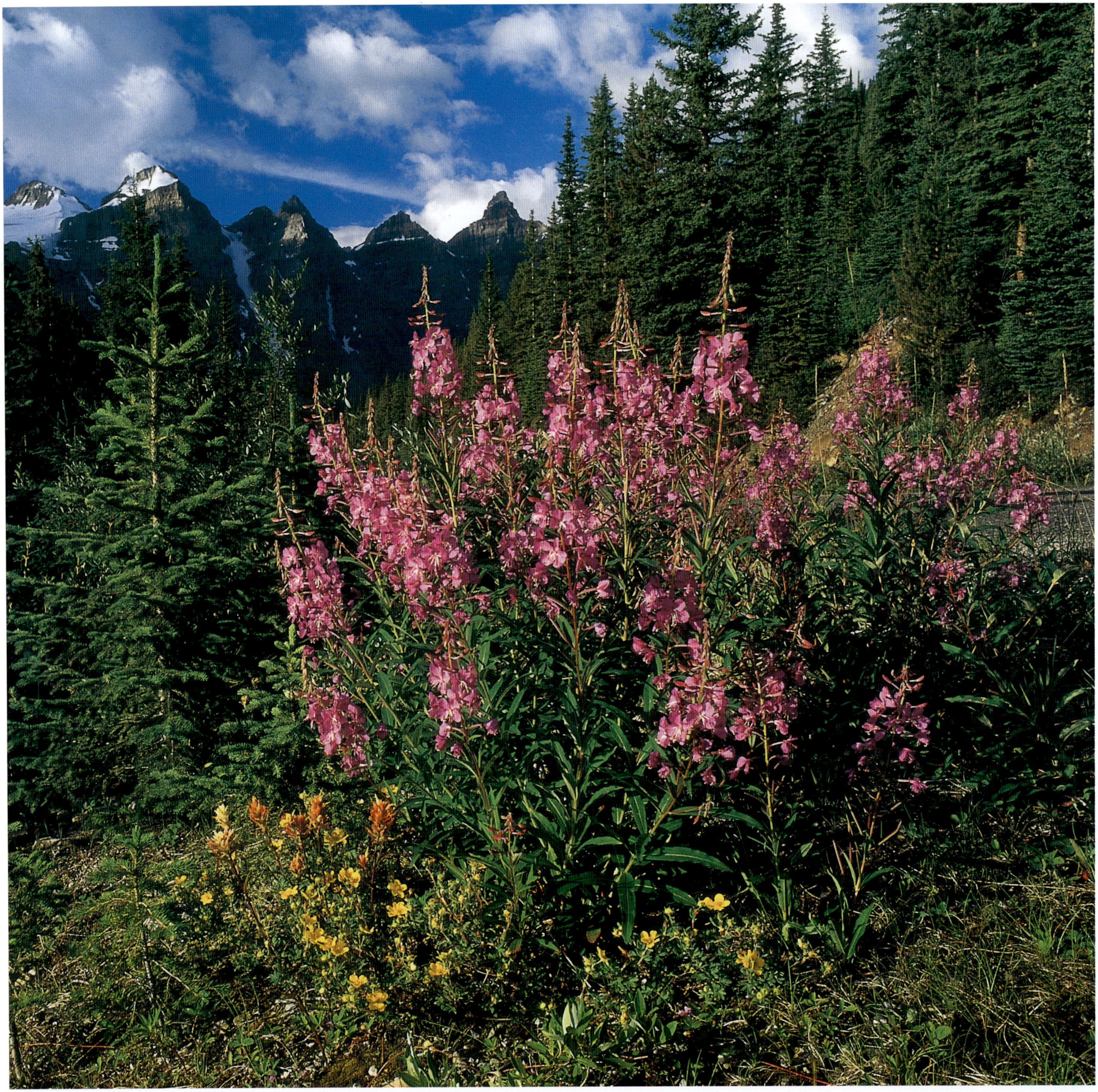

Looking down from Guinn Pass (2423m) towards Ribbon Lake – one of the sources of Ribbon Creek in Kananaskis Country. The very rugged south slopes of Mt. Bogart form a stark background.

Left: In a cozy, sheltered corner on the south slopes of Mt. Temple, a pretty clump of Fireweed (Epilobium ungustifolium) finds a hospitable environment in which to prosper. In the background are the distant peaks of the Valley of the Ten Peaks.

We are used to looking up at the mountains from the valley. In this instance, we look down on proud, lofty Castle Mountain (2766m), but not in contempt or disregard. One winter, the author happened to climb to the higher point to the north – Helena Ridge (2862m) and bivouacked overnight before taking this photo at first light. The Tower is on the left.

*W*apta Mountain (2778m) is located east of Emerald Lake, west of the Yoho River and north of the town of Field – being the northern extension of Mt. Field. This is not a hiking or scrambling hill – only climbers should attempt it. The climb is laborious and moderately difficult from any direction. The first party to reach the top, in 1901, was: J. Outram, J. Scattergood and C. Bohren. This photo features the rugged cliffs of the west face as seen from Mt. Burgess.

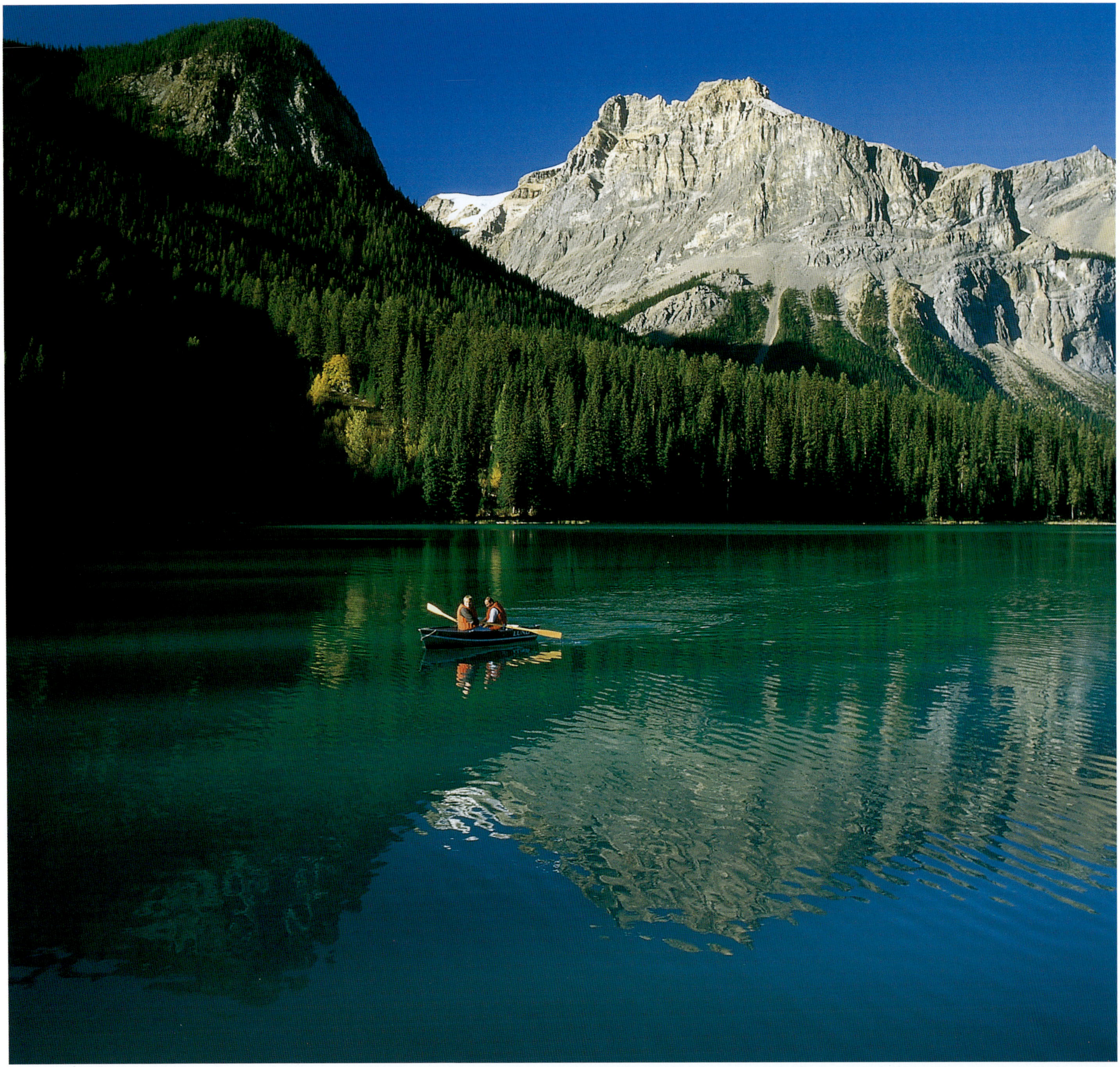

*T*he month of July is summer at its best in the Rockies. Visibly healthy and recovered winter's hardships, a majestic Elk (Cervus elaphus) enjoys a gourmet meal in a lush alpine meadow. His enormous, showy antlers still in velvet, will soon be ready for the rutting battles that begin in early September.

Left: *E*merald Lake, the gem of Yoho National Park, lives up to its name. The silty water is coming from the glacier-clad President Range to the north. The area is lush, green and rich in wildlife. Recreational possibilities are unlimited – from hiking to climbing to leisure canoeing.

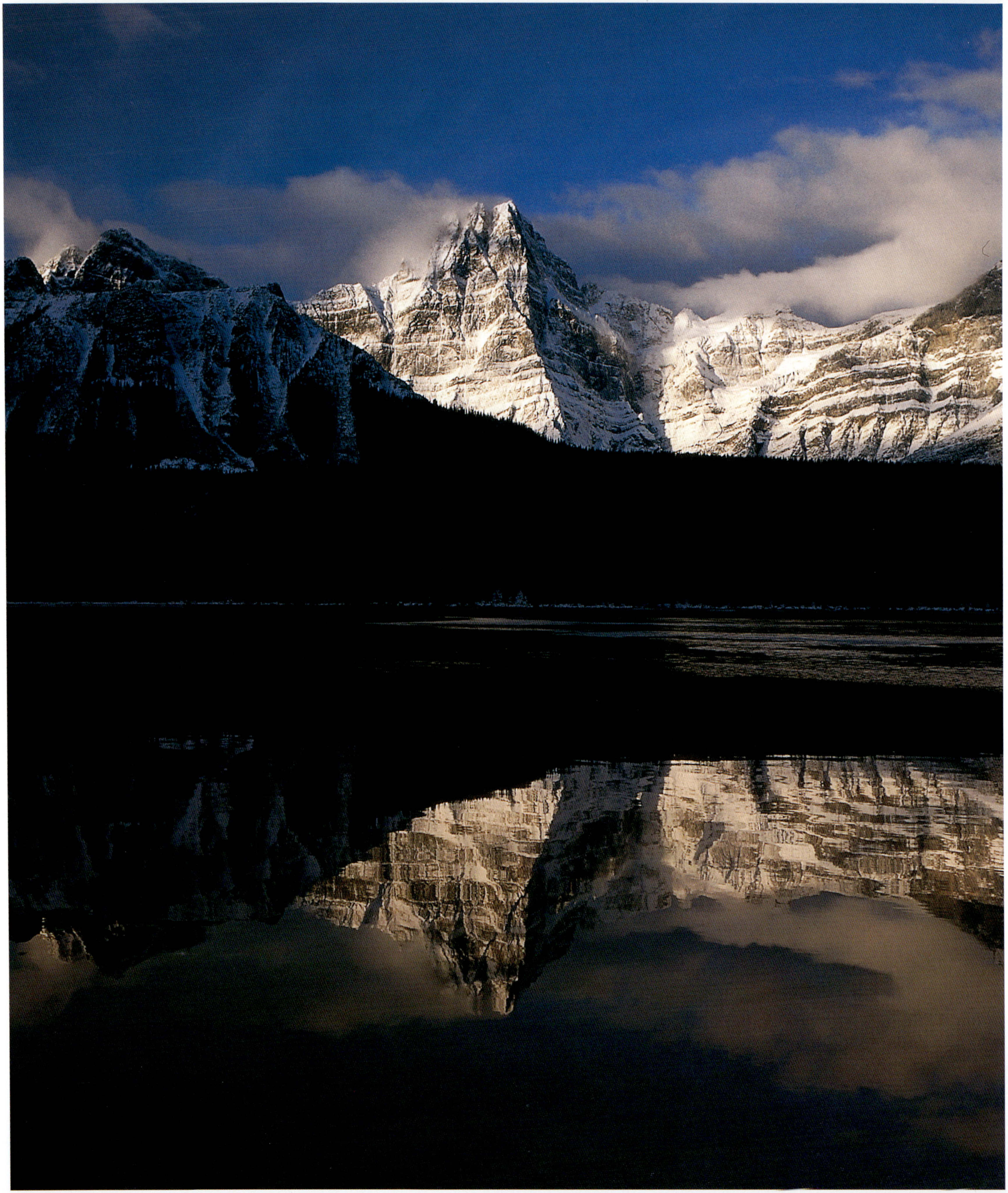

*T*he bulky, squat Mt. Temple (3543m) reflected in mirror-like Consolation Lake. That little hump on the left is the Tower of Babel, which is the northern extension of Mt. Babel. A beautiful, truly serene scene. Banff National Park.

Left: *A* moody morning on Upper Waterfowl Lake, Banff National Park. The lofty Howse Peak (3290m), of the Waputik Group, reflects its north face in the calm morning waters. The lake is a permanent summer home to a healthy Moose population.

Wintry Mt. Lefroy (3423) is a high, challenging mountain located east of the Abbot Pass and Mt. Victoria, and southwest of Lake Louise. The flamboyant, glacier-clad peak is named for John H. Lefroy, the former director of Magnetic Survey of Canada. It can be climbed from Lake Louise via the Victoria Glacier, or from Yoho's Lake O'Hara – both routes run via the Abbot Pass. Several very difficult routes from the east and north also exist.

A splendid sunrise creates the illusion of warmth and serenity. In reality, this tranquil December morning was cold, -25°C. This photo features the area along the Columbia Icefield. On the left is the Snow Dome, then Mt. Kitchener. The Athabasca Glacier is hidden behind the ridge on the left. This is the beautiful but cold reality of mountain winter. Jasper National Park.

The monarch of the Canadian Rockies – Mt. Robson (3954m) is the weather-maker, rain-catcher and creator of the area's microclimate. Here, the relatively dry Rockies receive a huge amount of precipitation, allowing a lush rainforest to thrive. Large Western Red Cedars and prickly Devil's Club plants adorn the photo.

*T*he Western Wood Lily (Lilium mountanum), a North American plant that averages 4-5 decimeters in height, is a showy orange-red with brown specks. It grows from bulbs and seeds in rather moist subalpine meadows, but can also be found in semi-dry areas. Picking the flower will cause the bulb to die and prevent its seeds from maturing. Please do not pick the flowers.

*F*airview Mountain (2744m) stands just south of Lake Louise. It is easily accessible by hiking trail to the Saddle followed by a short scramble to the northwest summit. The inspiring view encompasses, from the left: the north wall of Haddo Peak, Mt. Aberdeen and its north glacier, and Mt. Lefroy. In other directions, one can see Mt. Temple, Mt. Victoria, Mt. Whyte, Mt. Hector, the Bow Valley and, of course, Lake Louise. Banff National Park.

*W*aterton Lakes National Park is the only place where the Prairies meet the Rockies – no foothills here. The view from Mt. Alderson (2692m) looking east as the sun, rising over the Prairies, brings light and life – another day is born. On the left is Bertha Peak, in the center Middle Waterton Lake and on the right, Upper Waterton Lake. Spectacular scenery, except for that hexagon in the middle – the lens commercials claim that a super multi-coated lens will eliminate the hexagons?

An invigorating hike from Moraine Lake, up to Larch Valley, rewards one with a splendid view of Larch groves and a magnificent panorama of The Valley of the Ten Peaks. Late autumn, when the needles of the Larch turn gold, is the most enjoyable time to visit – Grizzlies permitting. The area is frequented by aggressive bears and is often closed for safety reasons.

It looks like one but this is not an aerial photo. The author sweated all the way to the summit of Pyramid Mountain (2766m) to photograph pristine, blue Pyramid Lake, just north of Jasper. It was a pleasant climb on a gorgeous autumn day. The views from here are surprisingly great in every direction – even Mt. Robson can be seen.

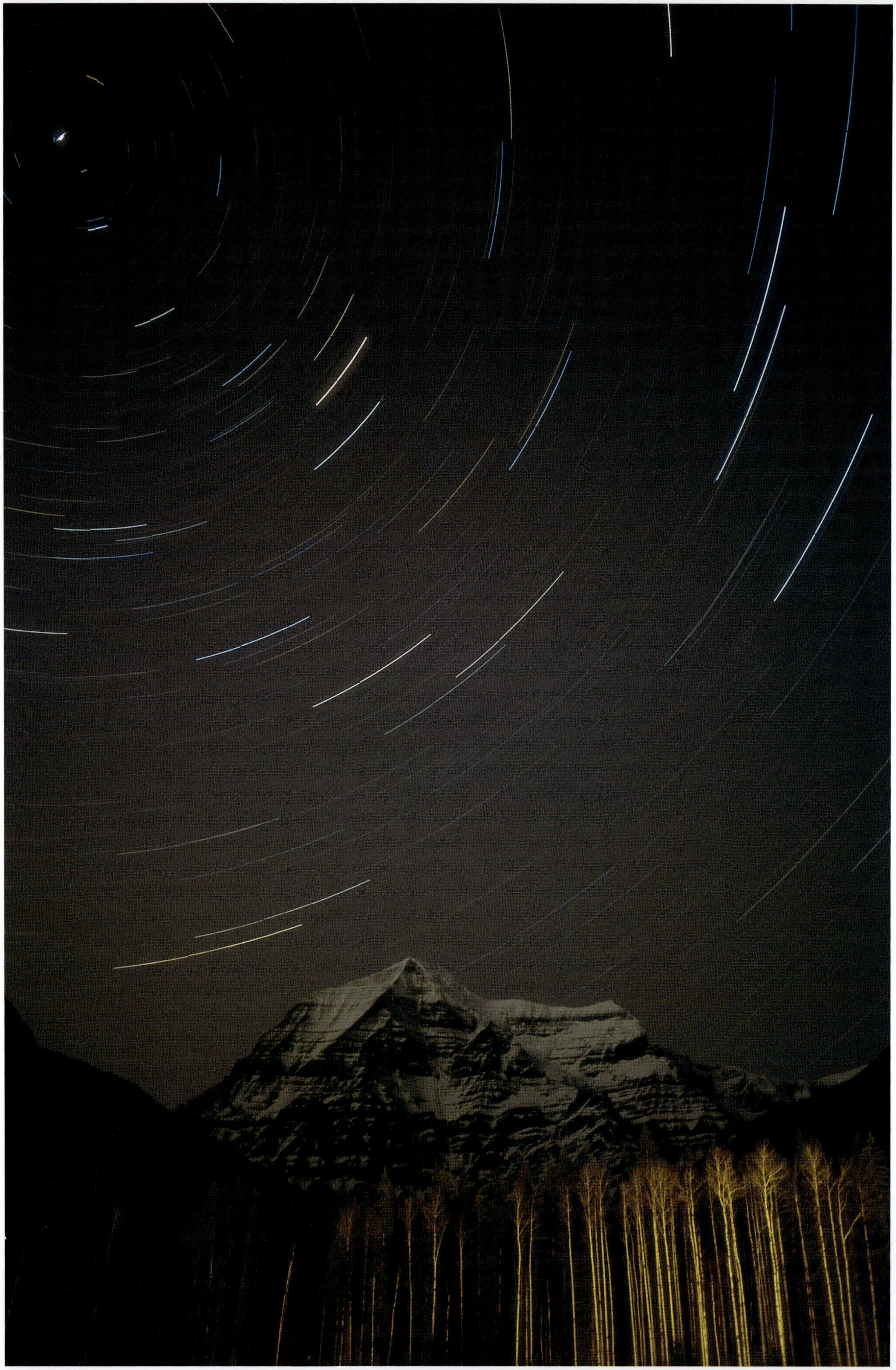

An unnamed peak (2750m) is located east of Baker Lake and south of Oyster Peak. This photo was taken from there, at Harvest Moon. On the left stands lofty Ptarmigan Peak (3059m), in the center is Fossil Mountain (2946m) and in the foreground, left, is Baker Lake and, further in the background, Ptarmigan Lake – just south of Deception Pass. Banff National Park.

Left: *A*utumn is a good time to photograph the night skies because the air is dry and the nights are long. Icecapped Mt. Robson (3954m) is located a little off-center to have a perfect symmetrical with Polaris above it photo. The 1.5-hour exposure registers star treks as Earth turns. Unfortunately, there were no shooting stars or meteorites but, fortunately, there were no airplanes or satellites passing by at the time of the exposure.

A glacier carved this little valley just southeast of Moraine Lake, Consolation Valley houses two lakes. Panorama Ridge flanks this beautiful, hidden valley to the east, Mt. Quadra to the south and Mt. Babel to the west. The valley is beautified by golden Larches, but is also frequented by unpredictable Grizzly Bears. Caution is advised.

Rainbows are quite common in flat areas. Mountain topography seems to interfere with the visibility of this colourful phenomenon. This photo was taken by Bow Falls, on the Bow River, as a ribbon of vivid colour adorns Mt. Rundle in the pouring rain on a July afternoon. An old cliche comes to mind: be in the right place, at the right time and one may get a great shot.

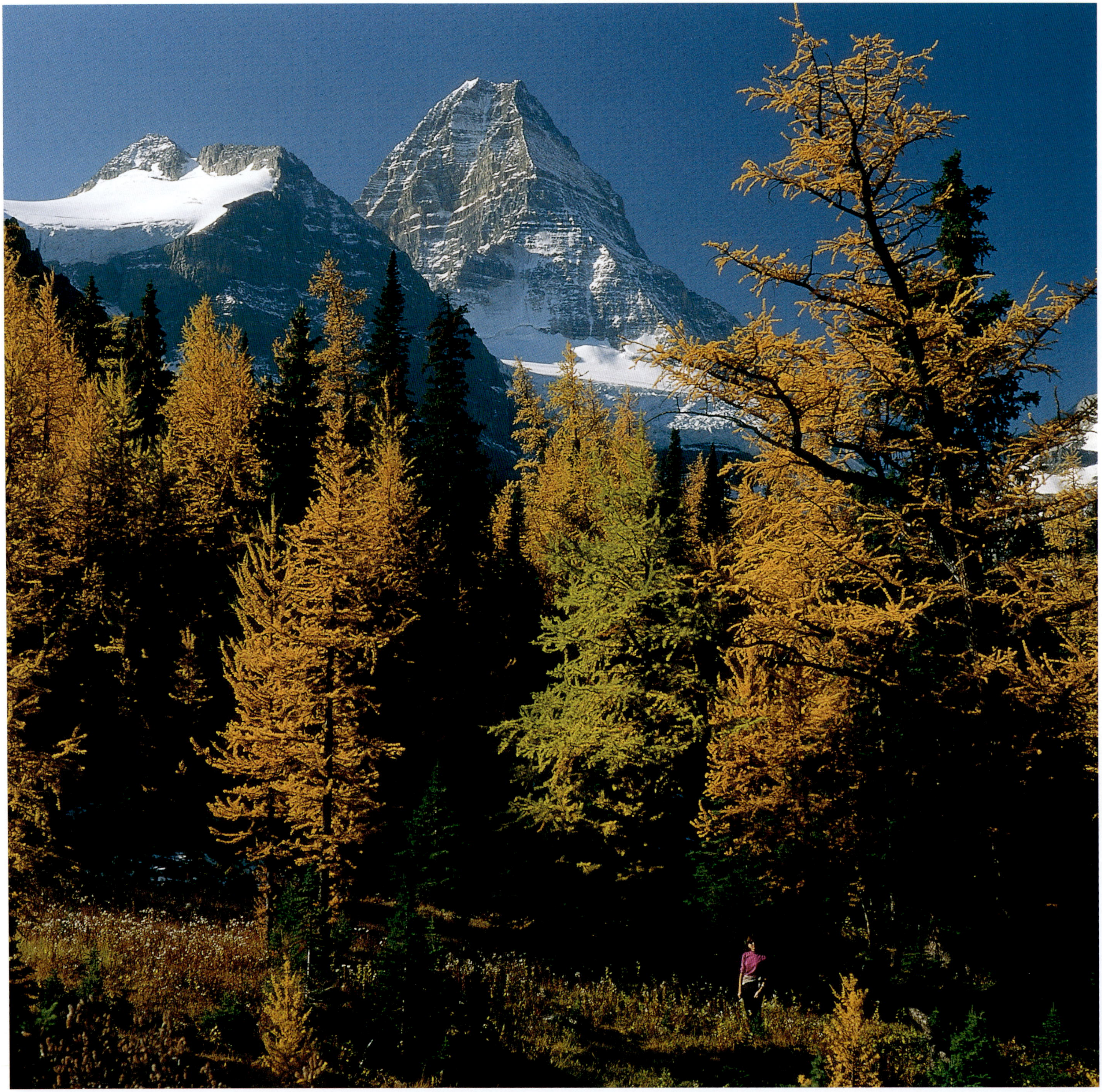

Before the fire, this forest was dense and dark and the forest floor had little vegetation. After the fire, the ash-enriched soil was quickly colonized by new plant life – mostly Fireweed (Epilobium angustifolium), which thrives on disturbed soil. It won't be long before the forest comes back, renewed and healthy – and the plant's on the forest floor will gradually vanish. It's nature's way.

Left: Mount Assiniboine Provincial Park, in eastern British Columbia, is a paradise of the first magnitude. Access is by hiking trail from Spray Lake or the Bourgeau road – both are over 20 km one-way. Perhaps the time is coming to upgrade this little paradise to National Park status because of its exceptional natural features and the need for more protection. Lofty Mt. Assiniboine (3618m) is the sixth-highest mountain in the Rockies.

40

High in the Vermilion Range, along an unnamed rock wall (3045m), the picturesque Floe Lake nestles in peace. A few hanging glaciers, lovely groves of Larch trees, lively meadows and a few Grizzlies dress up the surroundings. This photo was taken from the nub west of Numa Pass (2350m) at sunrise. Kootenay National Park.

Left: Camping is usually associated with lakeshore, a nice, warm campfire and plenty of good food. None of that could be enjoyed here, on the summit of Mt. Bourgeau (2930m) in the dead of winter. In the austere −20°C, it is not fun, but on the other hand, there were no mosquitoes at all! The rising sun casts 'warm', gentle hues on Mt. Brett on the left and Pilot Mountain. Banff National Park.

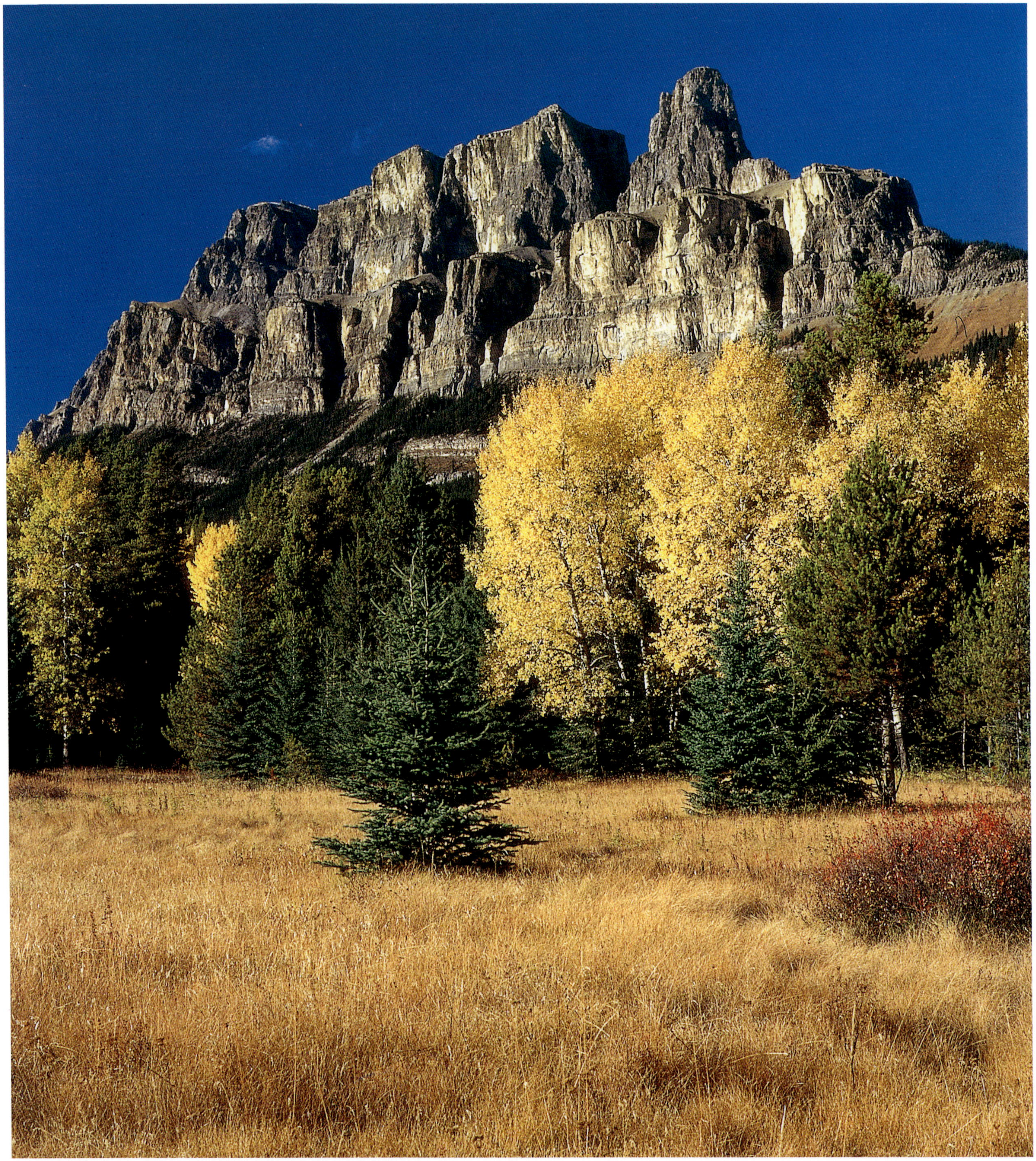

Adorned by the warm colours of golden autumn, the meadows along the Bow Valley bask in the sun of a glorious Alberta morning. Snow-clad Storm Mountain guards the Alberta – British Columbia border.

Left: The monumental Castle Mountain (2766m) is the guardian of the Bow Valley and the major landmark of Banff National Park. Photographed on a gorgeous autumn day, the mountain is surrounded by rich vegetation, forest and a diversity of fauna. It is a climber's paradise with a great variety of challenges.

The Northern Lights, also called Aurora Borealis, is a natural phenomenon that occurs in the circumpolar region of the north. In the Southern Hemisphere a similar phenomenon occurs and is called the Aurora Australis. It is caused by giant storms in the upper atmosphere. The Aurora performs a sinuous nocturnal dance – quickly or slowly depending on the intensity of the solar winds. The best time to view the Aurora is from November to March.

A celestial, nocturnal light show unfolds high above Castle Mountain (2766m) on a long autumn night. This two-hour exposure registered star treks as the Earth turned. The North Star, or Polaris, is almost stationary in the center. Some nights abound in meteorite showers, some do not. Here, a lone, small shooting star aims at Castle Mountain, but misses... by a few million kilometers. On the left horizon, the dying light of the sun still lingers, on the right, traces of the Aurora announces there is more to come later.

Autumn is a time of transition – leaves have fallen; temperatures plummeted; snow will soon replace rain and nature will rest peacefully beneath a thick blanket of white fluff. The grasshopper, immobilized by the cold, cannot jump so vigorously as in the summer. A magpie flew over the photographer's head several times as he photographed. Once he left, the magpie immediately claimed its prize – the grasshopper.

This lanky young Moose (Alces alces) is equipped with very long legs for good reason. The Moose finds the majority of its summer food under the water. Also, its long legs allow it to outrun predators like wolves or bears. But what if the Moose would like to dine on the lush grasses of the flats? Well, the Moose would hunker down on its knees and crawl from one clump of grass to another.

A misty mid-summer morning along the confluence of the Bow River and Mosquito Creek in Banff National Park. Because this is a higher elevation, flowers here are at their best by the end of July and into early August. Purple Willow-herbs and vivid red Indian Paintbrushes line the river.

A colourful palette of hues of wildflowers line Mosquito Creek in the central part of Banff National Park. The low morning sun richly highlights the colours and forms of the scene. Mosquito Creek measures only 10 km in length and originates in the valley east of Dolomite Peak.

Nothing cheers a weary hiker more than colourful, fragrant wildflowers, mingling here with spruce cones and wild strawberries. Summer at its best in the Canadian Rockies.

A change of colours in the second half of September announces the inevitable long, cold winter soon to come to the Valley of the Ten Peaks. Near-by Moraine Lake will soon freeze and then the white fluff of snow will cover the valley.

A peaceful scene of Two Jack Lake, just northeast of the town of Banff, with the northeast face of Mt. Rundle (2998m) reflected at first light of early summer as snow still lingers on the higher elevations. Banff National Park.

*T*he very rugged and dangerous walls on the east face of Cascade Mountain (2998m) in the Sawback Range – photographed at sunrise from Lake Minnewanka in early summer. First ascended in 1887 by the Stewart – Wilson team.

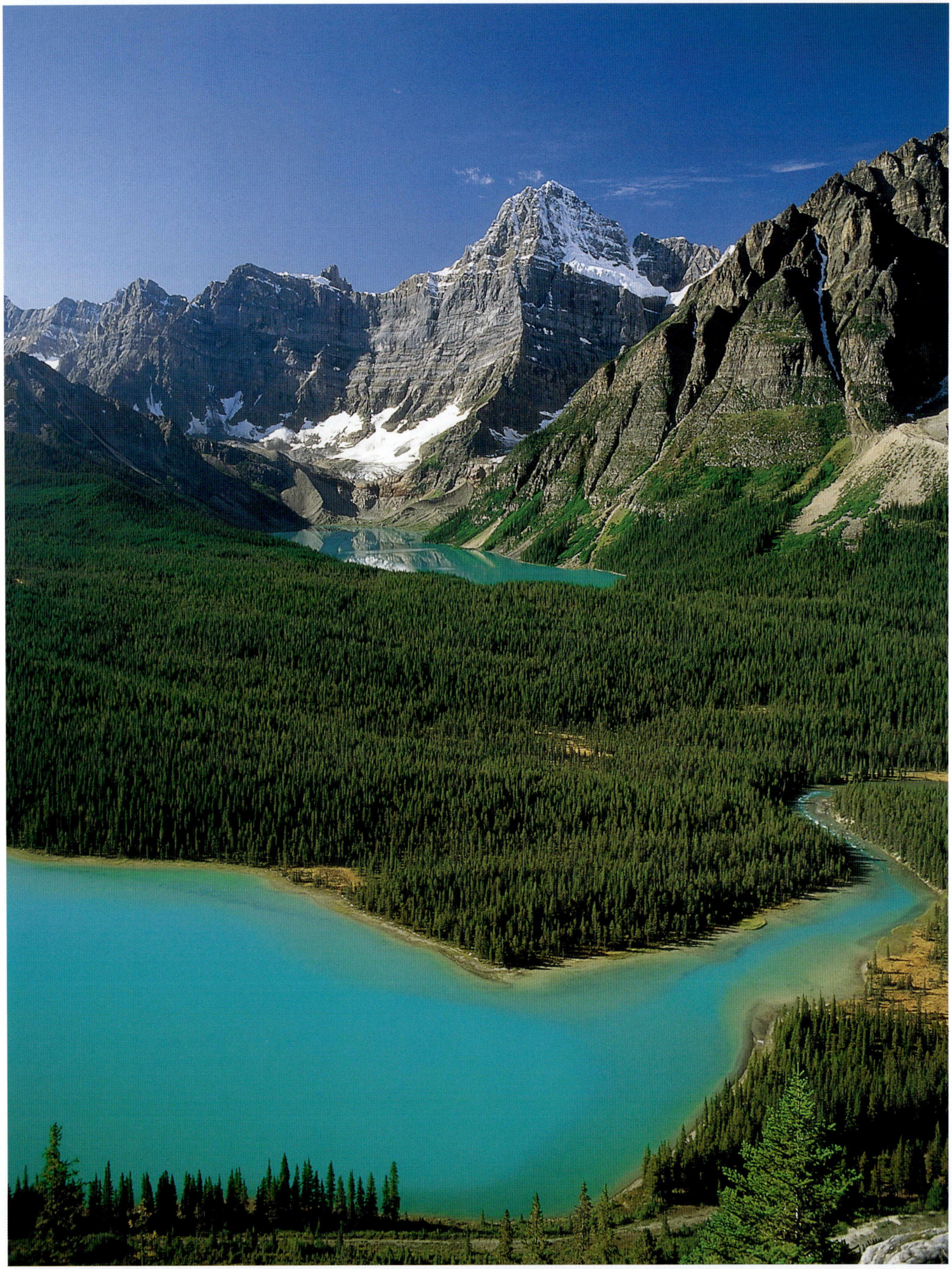

*L*arch Valley, just north of the Valley of the Ten Peaks, is the home of one of the largest concentrations of Larch Trees in the Rockies. The ice-capped Mt. Fay (3234m) graces the background. Mt. Fay is the first of the ten peaks by Moraine Lake and presents quite a challenge – especially at its ice covered northeast face. Banff National Park.

Left: *L*ower Waterfowl Lake is the emerald gem of the Mistaya Valley. Also emerald, is Chephren Lake, nestled at the foot of Howse Peak (3290m). Here the forest is pristine and healthy and provides a home for Grizzly Bears, Moose and other ungulates. A large number of waterfowl also spend the summer here.

Maligne Lake is the jewel of Jasper National Park. Many wonder how such a beautiful place got such an ominous name. The name was first given to the treacherous lower end of the Maligne River and then stuck to the lake as well. The lake is 22 km long and is flanked on both sides by great, glaciated mountains, many of which exceed an elevation of 3000m, and reaches the apex of the area – Mt. Brazeau (3470m) at the far end of the lake.

The turquoise Bow Lake nestles just east of the Great Divide, by Crowfoot Mountain (3050m). South of the lake sprawls the large Wapta Icefield and one of its many glaciers – the Bow Glacier, which gives birth to the Bow River – one of Alberta's great rivers. Moose, Bears and numerous waterfowl can be seen at the east end of the lake. Seldom is a large body of water, like this, so calm – allowing a nearly perfect reflection.

The exuberant, lush, pristine rainforest sprawls around the highest mountain in the Canadian Rockies – Mt. Robson (3954m).

Originating at the Winkchemna Glacier, the clear water of Moraine Creek runs down to join the Bow River. Banff National Park.

The clearly defined upper limit of vegetation in the mountains is quite obvious. Nothing grows higher than the climate allows. Even if some seeds would germinate in a cold, wrong place and survive for a year or two, the harsh climate would eventually destroy them. Here on Opal Peak, north of Maligne Lake, summer rain turned into snow at the top – where the temperature is 15°C colder than at the base. Jasper National Park.

The popularity of mountain climbing systematically grows in Canada, year by year. In summer or winter, Mt. Athabasca (3490m) is always fair game for adventurers. Starting at 5 a.m., a group of six climbers (in the shadow at right) hope to reach the summit in five hours, have time to explore the mountain and make a leisurely return – as the long July day allows. Banff/Jasper National Parks.

*G*eologists speculate that, many moons ago, a rockslide from Mt. Babel tumbled down to block Moraine Creek and create Moraine Lake. Others say that in the upper valley, a rockslide fell on the Winkchemna Glacier, was carried down by the moving ice until it melted and the rocks blocked the creek. Both speculations are possible, but all agree that Moraine Lake is the prime emerald gem of the Rockies and this photo confirms that beyond a doubt.

*L*ocated just east of the Great Divide, Lake Louise receives enough summer precipitation to keep the area lush and green. Winter brings heavy snowfall, as the area is within the so-called 'snow belt', which is quite clearly defined. One place gets as much as 5 meters of snow, while one kilometer further; the snowfall is only 2 meters. Photographed through the December morning mist, Mt. Whyte (2983m) stands guard by the lake. Mt. Victoria and Lake Louise are on the left.

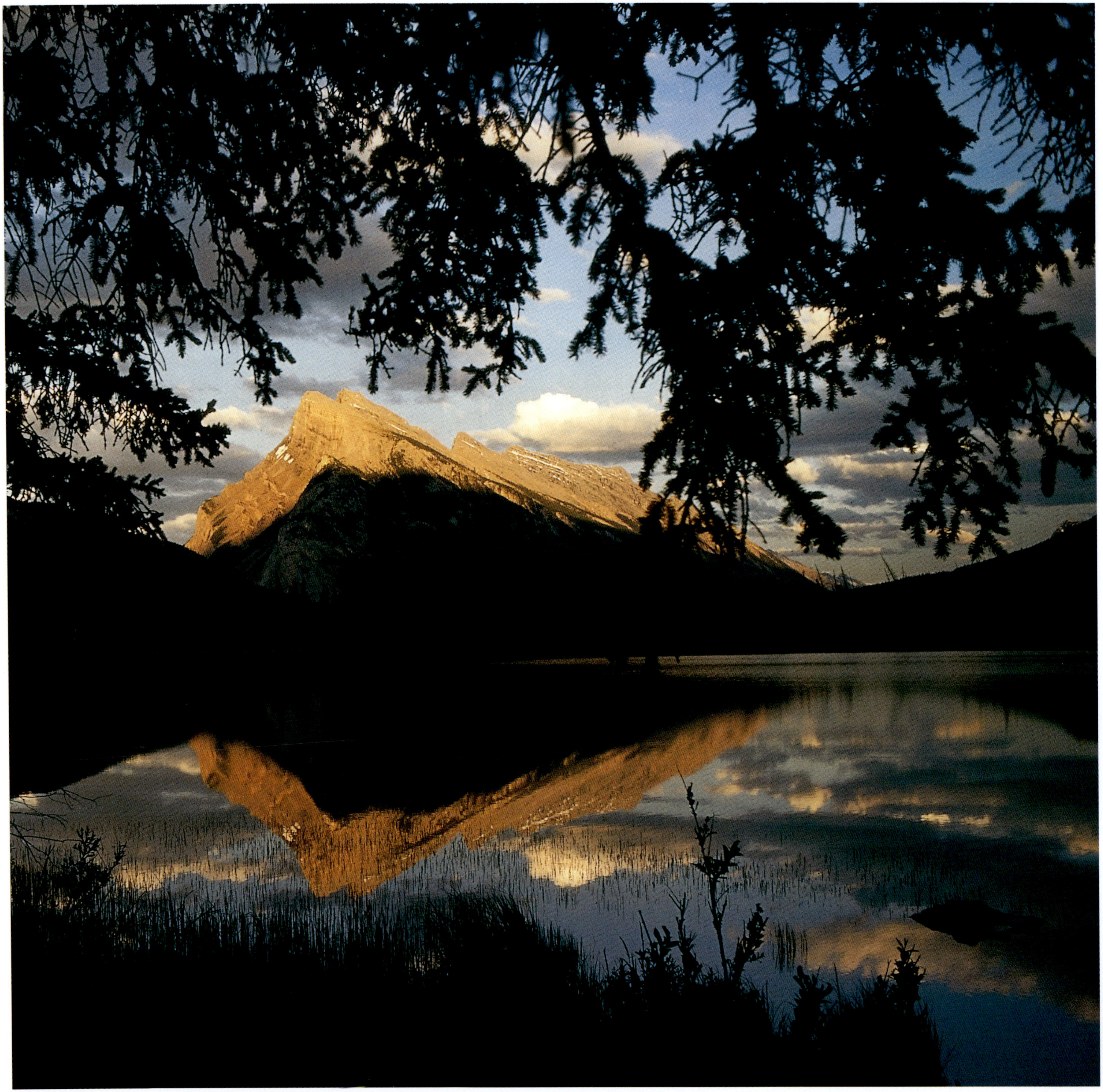

*P*hotography is an art. Just as a painter puts colour and shape on a canvas, the photographer must first see the subject and then approach it from the proper angle. Take three photographers to the same location and let them shoot. Most likely, each will come up with very different images. Here is a neat composition: autumn poplars growing on a mountain, beneath the sun and clouds.

Left: *I*t is good to realize that a well run National Park does protect nature very adequately. The Three Vermilion Lakes are just minutes from the busy town of Banff, yet the area appears to be quite undisturbed. The lakes are full of fish and waterfowl; the Bald Eagle and Osprey make their homes here. Elk, Deer, Bears, Wolves and Coyotes frequent the area. Only the Moose is permanently missed. Mt. Rundle (2998m) is reflected in the First Vermilion Lake.

In the far north's hostile climate, the Igloo was the winter home for the Eskimo people (now called Inuit) for thousands of years. Built from large blocks of hard snow, which is a good insulator, when its 'front door' is closed and a few people are inside, the temperature soon rises to above freezing. When any heat source, even a candle is used, the temperature will rise from 5 – 10°C. Not bad, when the outside temperature might be –40°C, with a full-blown blizzard raging. The author builds Igloos every winter.

The beautiful, turquoise Bow Lake takes a seven-month break and rests peacefully under a heavy blanket of white fluff. Bow Lake and Crowfoot Mtn (3050m) are located at the north edge of the Wapta Icefield and its numerous glaciers. Bow Glacier is the source of the Bow River. Banff National Park.

A gorgeous August evening along Mosquito Creek – a perfect time to sit down and read a book, or just admire the scenery. Cheery purple Willow-herbs line the shore as Mt. Andromache (2996m) looks on. A nearby campground and youth hostel provide rustic accommodations.   Banff National Park.

While exploring a little creek, the author stumbled onto a colourful "bouquet" of wildflowers in its middle. It looked so neat, he shot two frames but it was after dusk and too dark. On his return, it looked even better – a dream-like stream, so he shot another three frames – using a ten-second exposure because of the darkness. Never mind the conditions – always take the shot and see what turns out.

Rushing down over rocks and boulders, and along moraines, these icy waters come from the northern glacier of Mt. Athabasca and the Athabasca and Dome Glaciers – the source of the Sunwapta River. The area is known as the Columbia Icefield – which is south of here on a high plateau about 10 km away. Mt. Athabasca is on the left, Mt. Andromeda is in the center and the Athabasca Glacier is on the right.

An early morning view of Peyto Lake, photographed from a high ridge southeast of the lake. It is named for an early guide, explorer and all-around colourful character – Bill Peyto. On the left stands Caldron Peak (2917m), which can be climbed from the east or scrambled from the west side. The Bow Summit area is a home to Grizzly Bears. The author had two brushes with them – one nearly fatal.

Emerald Lake is a world-famous gem of Yoho National Park and accessible by paved road year round. Many pleasant hikes and climbs can be enjoyed in the area, as well as water sports and cross-country skiing. Mt. Burgess (2599m) stands guard south of the lake – its northwest face presents a major climbing challenge. The mountain can be ascended via a broken northeast ridge quite easily, but it is a labourious long climb.

*C*amping is not permitted just anywhere – only in designated campgrounds. "Winter camping" on Moraine Lake was staged for this picture and then "the campers" skied back to Lake Louise on a cold but pleasant, moonlit night. The ice crystals in the air caused the photo's lack of sharpness, but overall, the image is pleasant. The author skis to Moraine Lake at least twice every winter and finds the trips very enjoyable.

Walking along a mountain creek, or stream, one can see dozens of waterfalls of varying sizes – cascading waters, small pools and so forth. Lush vegetation is always present along these life-giving waters. Photographing the lively waters is always an enjoyable, learning experience.

The majestic Bighorn Sheep (Ovis canadensis) are quite common in the Rockies. They are often seen begging for handouts along the road. Please do not feed the wildlife – not only is it illegal, it also contributes to the deaths of many animals on the roads.

In the upper part of Johnston Creek, interesting rock forms attract the keen eye of the photographer. An oversized "Club of Hercules" stands in the water and is eroded by the elements and time. Hundreds, or thousands of years from now, it will surely fall and perhaps create a small lake. Nature at work – history written in the rock. Banff National Park.

*T*he glacier-carved Consolation Valley, and Lower and Upper Consolation Lakes, are a short, pleasant walk from Moraine Lake. The Panorama Ridge to the east, Mt. Babel to the west and Mt. Quadra flank the valley on the south. The valley was photographed from the Tower of Babel, in adverse light as a storm fast approached from the west. Banff National Park.

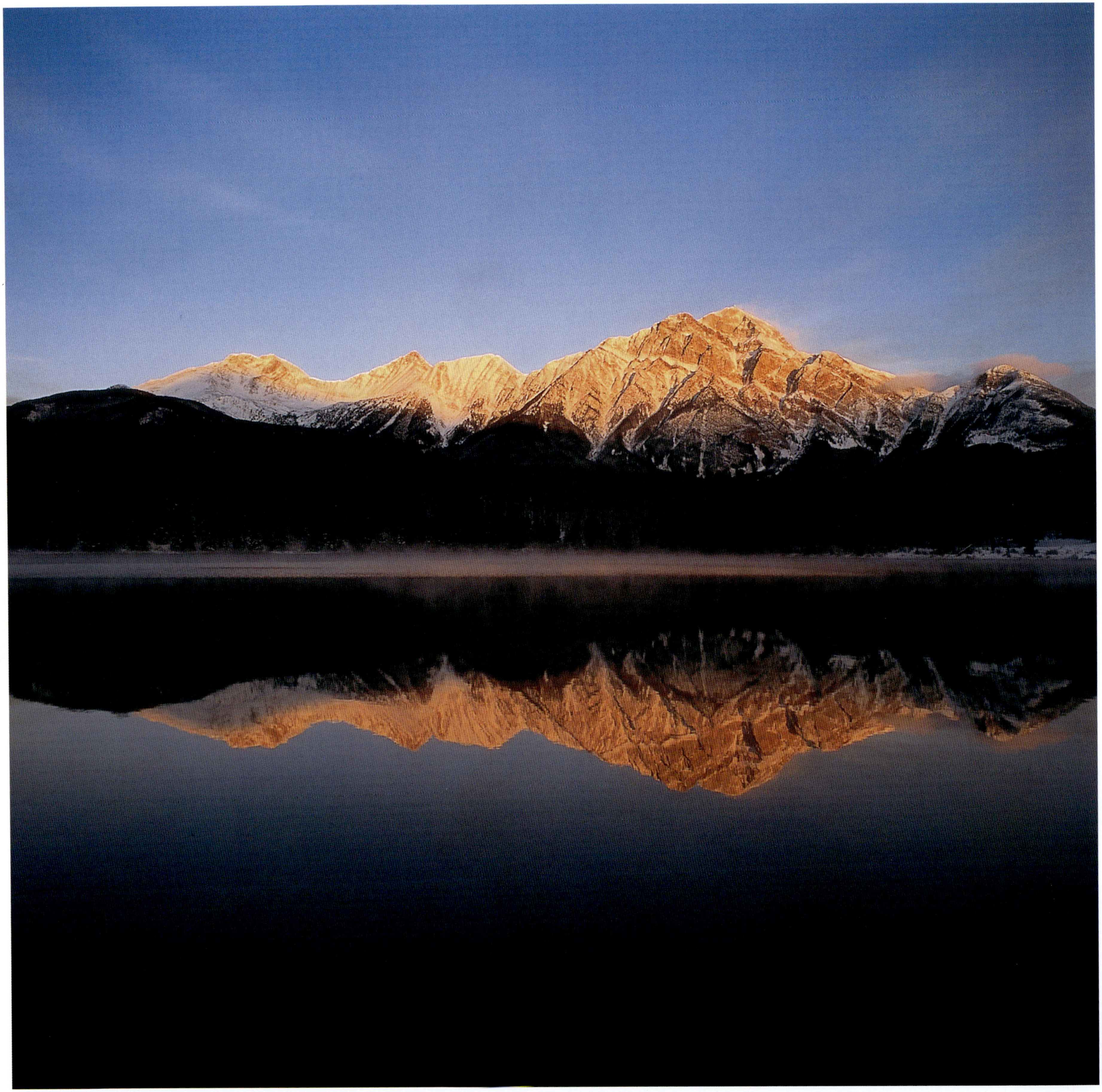

Along the Icefields Parkway, between the North Saskatchewan River and Rampart Creek, looms the huge Mt. Wilson (3261m), which stretches almost 10 km. The mountain is home to a large colony of sheep and goats, and its north side is heavily glaciated. J. Outram, guided by C. Kaufmann, was the first to climb it, in 1902.

Left: Dusted by the first late autumn snow, Pyramid Mountain (2766m) reflects its east face on the misty Patricia Lake. The Patricia is one of many lakes in the Jasper area and Pyramid Mountain, of the Victoria Cross Range, is a dominant landmark north of Jasper. The area is home to a large variety of wildlife – hundreds of Elk choose the area for their winter range.

"*S*omewhere over the rainbow..." the huge Takakkaw Falls (Native Canadian for splendid) rushes its icy waters down to the Yoho River. The drop is over 300m, the waters come from a high plateau at the west end of the Waputik Icefield and the Daly Glacier. The best time to view this spectacle is in early summer, when the snow and ice are quickly melting. Yoho National Park.

The Banff area seems to be the rainbow capitol of the Rockies. The rainbow phenomenon occurs when rain falls across the sky from the sun's location low on the horizon. The rainbow's colours are an artist's palette. From the three basic colours: red, yellow and blue, the rainbow combines them to create red, orange, yellow, green, blue, indigo and violet.

A fine example of pristine nature which, while exposed to substantial human activity, is strictly protected by its National Park Status. The southeastern slopes of Mt. Temple present rich meadows and healthy forests. Banff National Park.

The showy perennial herb Flea-Bane (Erigeron peregrinus) in late summer. It is closely related to genus Aster and is not clearly differentiated from it. In the Canadian Rockies it can be found in high alpine meadows and may reach 40 cm in height and 5 cm in diameter.

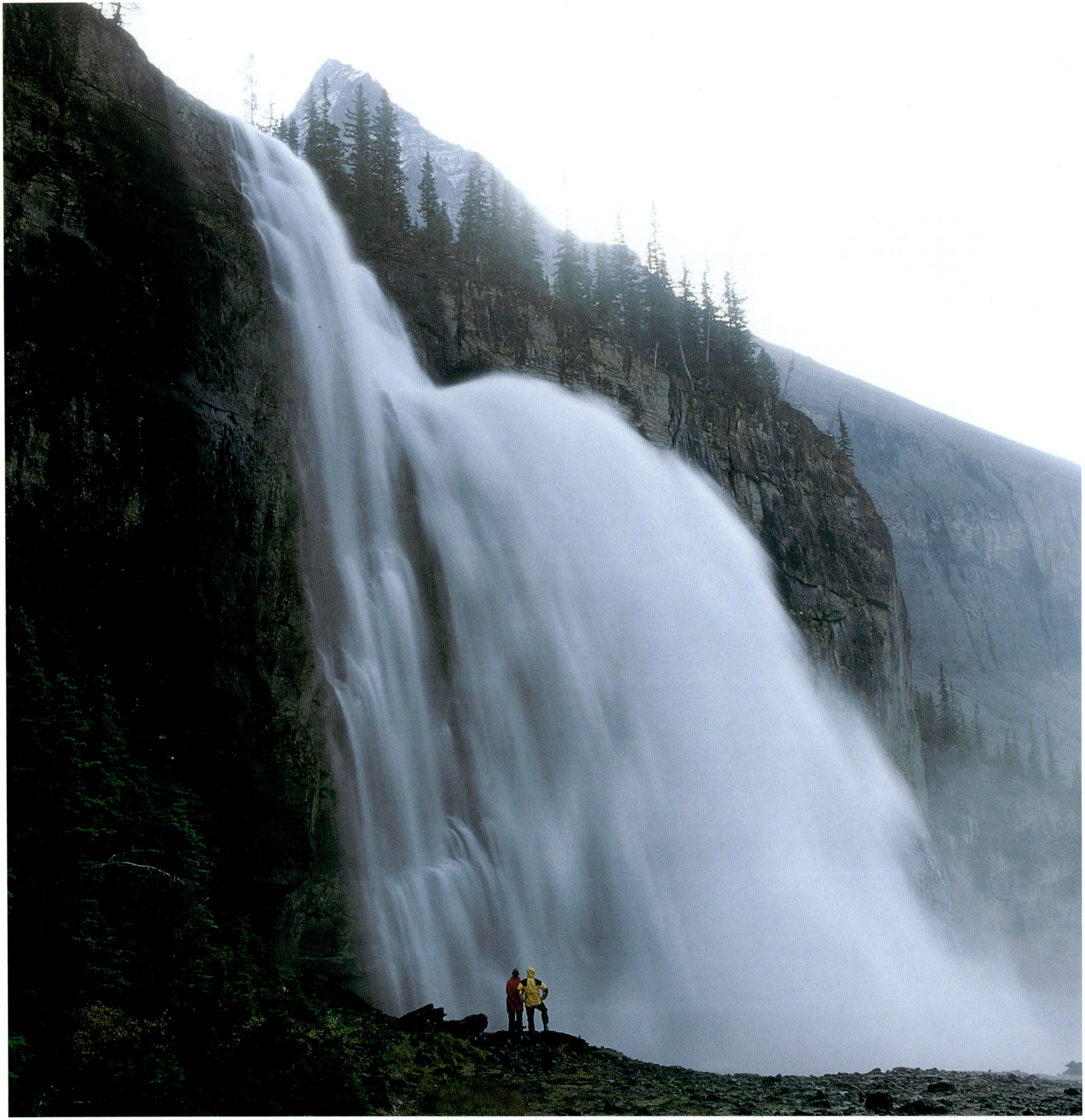

This picture is not out of focus – the weather is! A vicious blizzard blows, snow swirls and the wind howls like a pack of hungry wolves along the Rockies' foothills near Waterton. Surely no man or beast would go out in weather like that? For a Badger, however, it was business as usual – as it was for a well-seasoned photographer who put on his 400mm lens and ran after the Badger. The animal disappeared as quickly as it appeared and the cold and numb photographer came back empty-handed.

Left: When melting snow is at its height in early summer, the Emperor Falls, on the Robson River below Berg Lake, is quite impressive. On the north side of Mt. Robson (3954m) there are several large glaciers and snowfields that contribute water for the falls. These two 'little' people are over six feet tall but are overwhelmed by the size of the Emperor Falls. The top of Mt. Robson and the Emperor Ridge form the background.

The wintry northeast face of Mt. Chephren (3266m), also known as the Black Pyramid, basks in the morning sun. Behind it is the slightly higher, glacier-clad White Pyramid (3275m). Both are moderately difficult to climb. Chephren was first climbed in 1913 and the White Pyramid in 1939. Banff National Park.

The magic of light created this sparkling fairytale image. This is not a waterfall on a creek or river; this is snow-melt water running down the slopes in early summer. Yoho National Park. Here, one can listen to the soothing sounds of the water and enjoy the intricate beauty of nature.

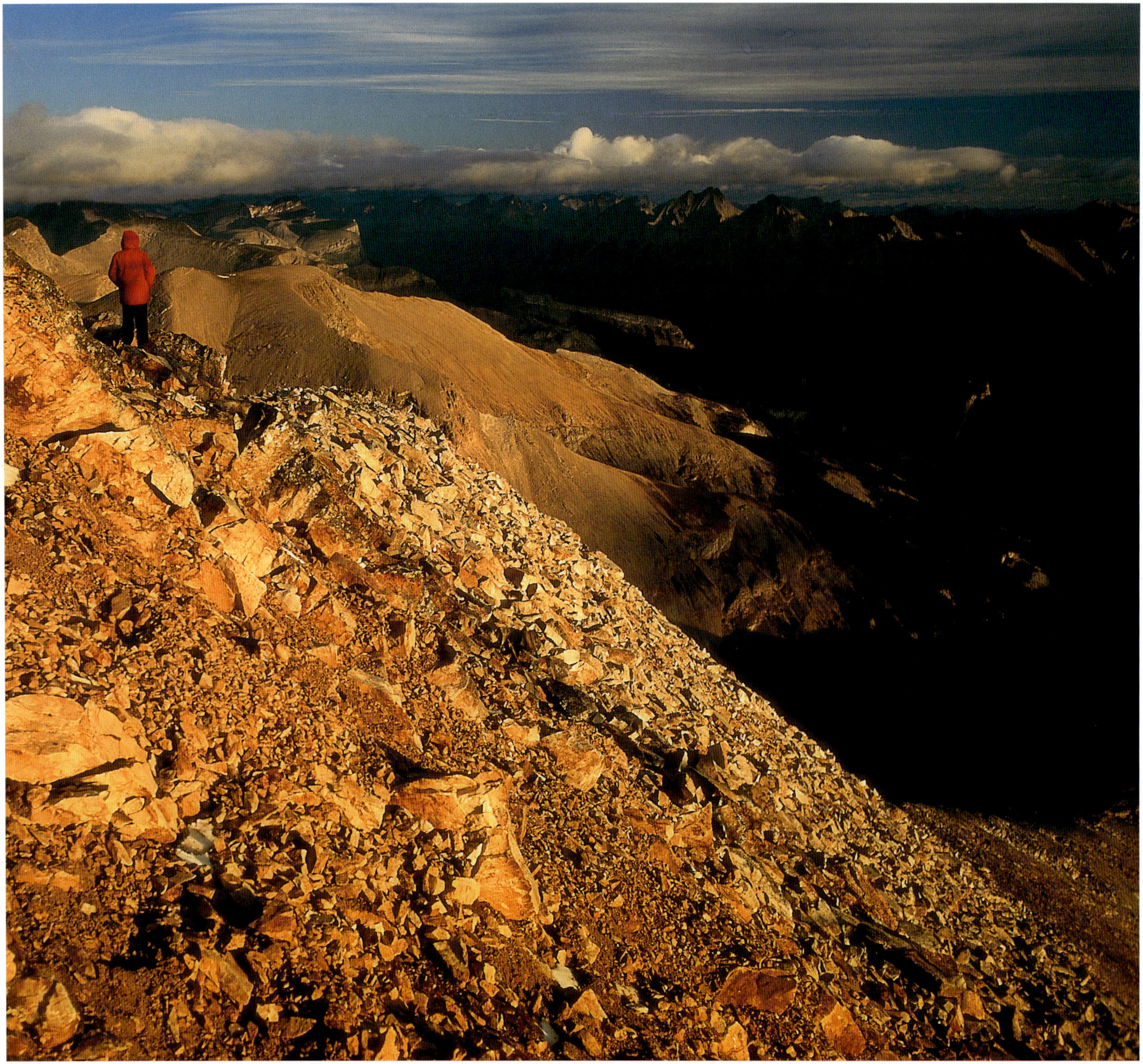

Another fabulous sunrise on the summit of Mt. Athabasca (3490m), looking south. The foreground features the east glacier of Mt. Andromeda and the middle-ground presents Mt. Castleguard (3077m), the southeast apex of the Columbia Icefield. Banff/Jasper National Parks. The three peaks of the giant Mt. Bryce (3507m) dominate the horizon, the west peak being the highest – a major climbing challenge by any standard.

Left: *An invigorating hike from Pyramid Lake, north of Jasper, gets one to the back of Pyramid Mountain (2766m). Then a fairly easy scramble, on good rock, gets one to the summit. A huge microwave station occupies the entire summit. From here, sweeping views can be enjoyed in all directions – even lofty Mt. Robson is clearly visible. This photo was taken at sunrise and features the view to the north. Jasper National Park.*

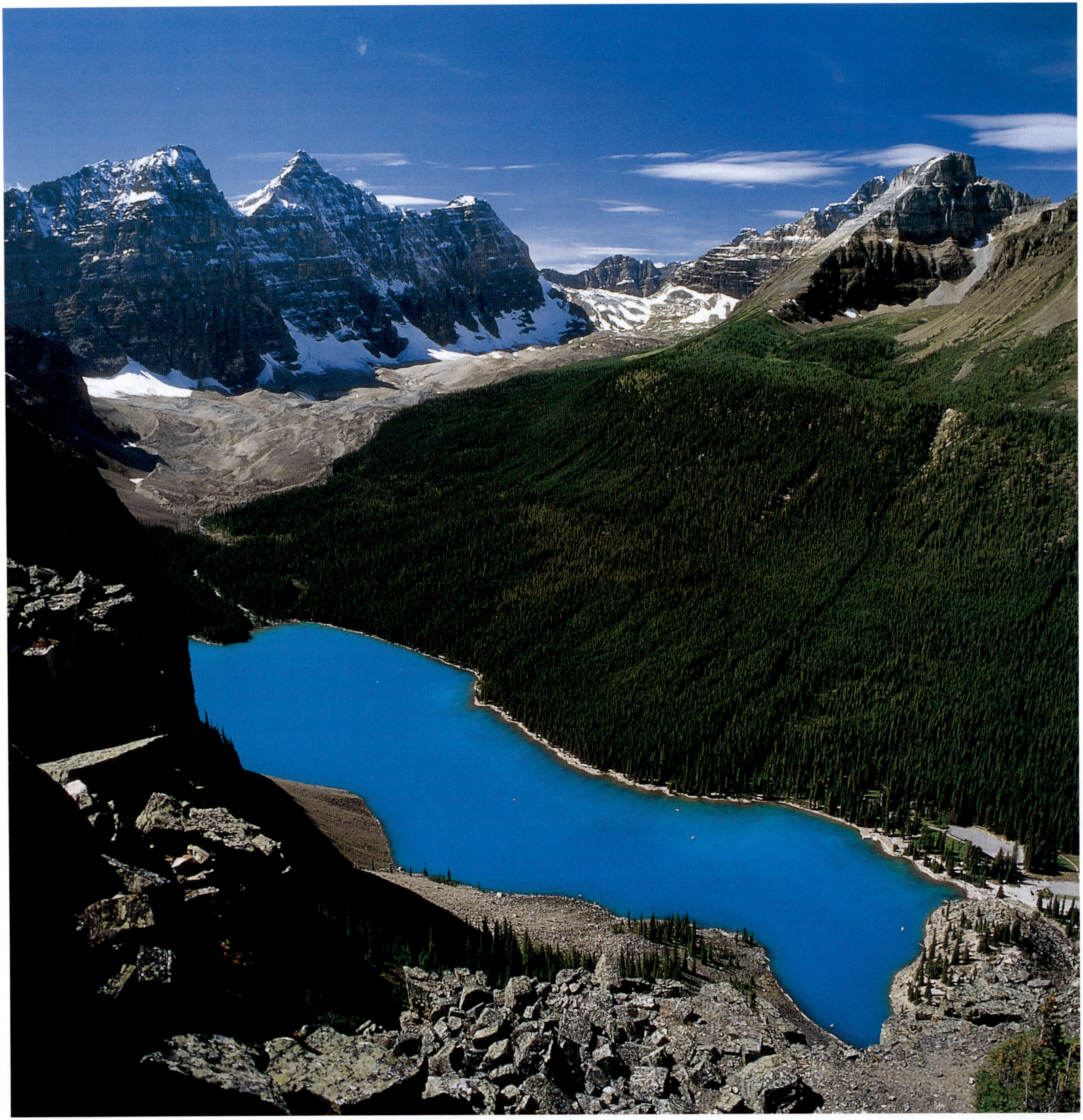

*T*he enchanted wilderness of the Valley of the Ten Peaks is as beautiful as ever. Mt. Quadra is at left, Mt. Babel dominates the center and a few of the "Ten Peaks" follow. Flowers fluctuate in size and appearance from year to year. When a plant is 'tired', or climatic conditions are unfavourable, the flowers are small and scruffy, or nonexistent. Then, rested and invigorated, they come back lush and beautiful the following year.

Left: *C*limbing the Tower of Babel, by Moraine Lake, is a good workout – beneficial for body and mind. A breathtaking view of Moraine Lake, the Valley of the Ten Peaks, Consolation Valley and Mt. Temple comes as a fine bonus. The incredible colour of the lake is due to its glacial water coming from the Winkchemna Glacier, visible on the left. Most of the glacier is covered by gravel and rock fallen from the peaks on the left, which makes the glacier dangerous, as many crevasses are hidden.

This is a three-hour, multiple exposure of the moon over Herbert Lake, just northwest of Lake Louise. Nocturnal wonders that could be called a string of shining pearls on the neck of the cosmos, or simply, a moonlight sonata. The clear skies, calm waters – and no ducks to make ripples – allowed for taking this quite decent photo.

*A*long the Rockies' foothills, summer thunderstorms are a common occurence. Thunderstorms are a result of highly electrified clouds and are often associated with heavy rain. The discharge of that power occurs in a flash, or very large spark and that is what we call lightning. Lightning may target another cloud, or the earth.

Another summer storm approaches Bow Summit (2069m) and its flowery meadows. In the next few minutes, summer turns to winter as a few centimeters of snow fall in the high country in August. The storm was gone in half an hour and the strong summer sun melted the snow in a few hours. The hardy and resilient mountain flowers were not much affected.

Goat's Beard (Tragopogon dubius) is commonly found along the foothills and lower Rockies. It is not native to this land, but since it has grown here for a long time, we might as well accept it as such. There are over fifty species of Tragopogon worldwide, mostly in Euro-Asia. The name comes from the Greek: Tragos – goat, pogon – beard. On the subject of flowers: in today's greatly endangered ecology, we must take extra care of any 'green things'. We must not pick flowers, plants or trees without need. Once they are destroyed, we cannot bring them back.

The Ramparts is a beautifully rugged, remote range of mountains about 15 km long and located on the west flank of the Tonquin Valley, south of Jasper. The snow and ice of the surrounding mountains and the two Amethyst Lakes are the source of the Astoria River. The pristine and healthy ecosystem provides sufficient environment for rich flora and fauna – from Blue Lupins to Grizzly Bears and Mountain Caribou. Photographed from Mt. Clitheroe at sunrise. Jasper National Park.

*T*he western part of The Ramparts, dominated by Bastion Peak, Turret Mtn. and Mt. Geikie (3308m), with the north Amethyst Lake in the foreground – the distant Moat Lake and Tonquin Creek, which flow west to join the Fraser River, are on the right. This splendid paradise was photographed from Mt. Clitheroe, east of the scene. How do you get here? The Tonquin Valley is accessible by two major trails: Mt. Edith Cavell road and the Marmot Basin road. Both trips are over 20 km one way and not recommended for a one-day hike. All of this area, and especially the Maccarib Pass, is home to Grizzly Bears.

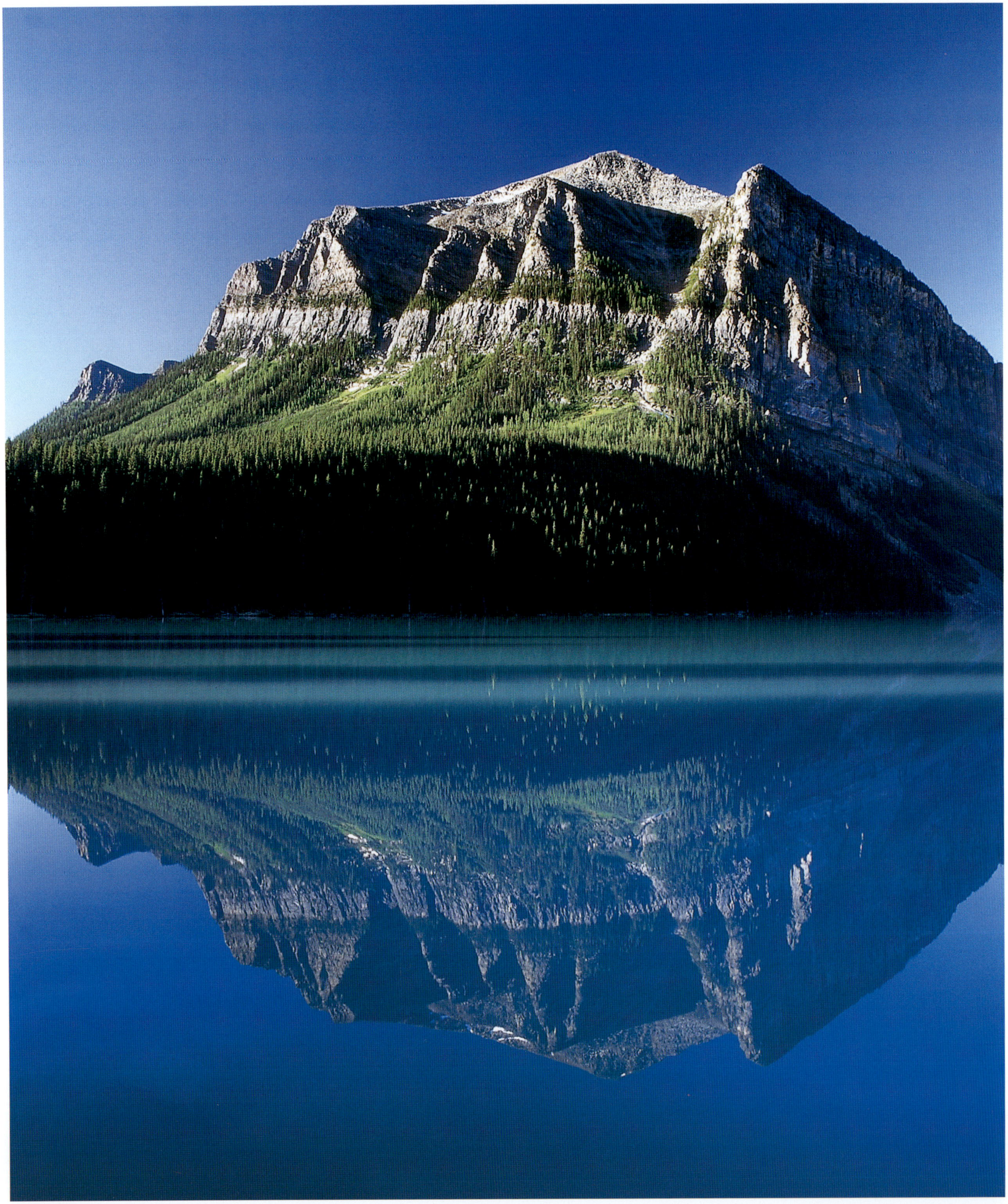

A mountain creek has a life of its own. The water does what it always does – rushes down to join a bigger creek, then a river, then a larger river and finally empties into the ocean. Rain, snow and ice meltwaters from upper reaches drain into valleys, giving life to all along its way: plants, beasts and man. Here, Helen Creek, which originates at Helen Lake, near the Dolomite Pass, rushes down to join the Bow River.

Left: Does this image resemble Lake Louise? Where is the patented postcard view of glaciated Mt. Victoria? This photo does, indeed, feature Lake Louise and reflected in it, Fairview Mtn (2744m) , flanking the lake on the south side. The early morning light, long shadows, the September chill and a wide-angle lens make for a very pleasant image.

The author's specialty has always been bivouacking on mountaintops. Here we see him 'enjoying' a great morning atop Mt. Temple (3543m). In late September, with the wind chill factor, the temperature drops to −25°C. After taking a few photos at sunrise, the author huddles in his sleeping hole to warm up and then takes more photos. Horseshoe Glacier and the surrounding peaks provide a splendid backdrop. Banff National Park.

The Forbes-Outram Group is located between the Glacier and Howse Rivers and north of the Freshfield Group. This very large group – about 100sq.km – features Mt. Forbes (3612m), the seventh highest mountain of the Rockies, large glaciers and many climbing routes. In the foreground, on the left, is the wintry Howse River Valley, with its rich forest, where wildlife abounds. It is not unusual to encounter several Bears on the way up beyond Glacier Lake or the Howse Pass. Banff National Park.

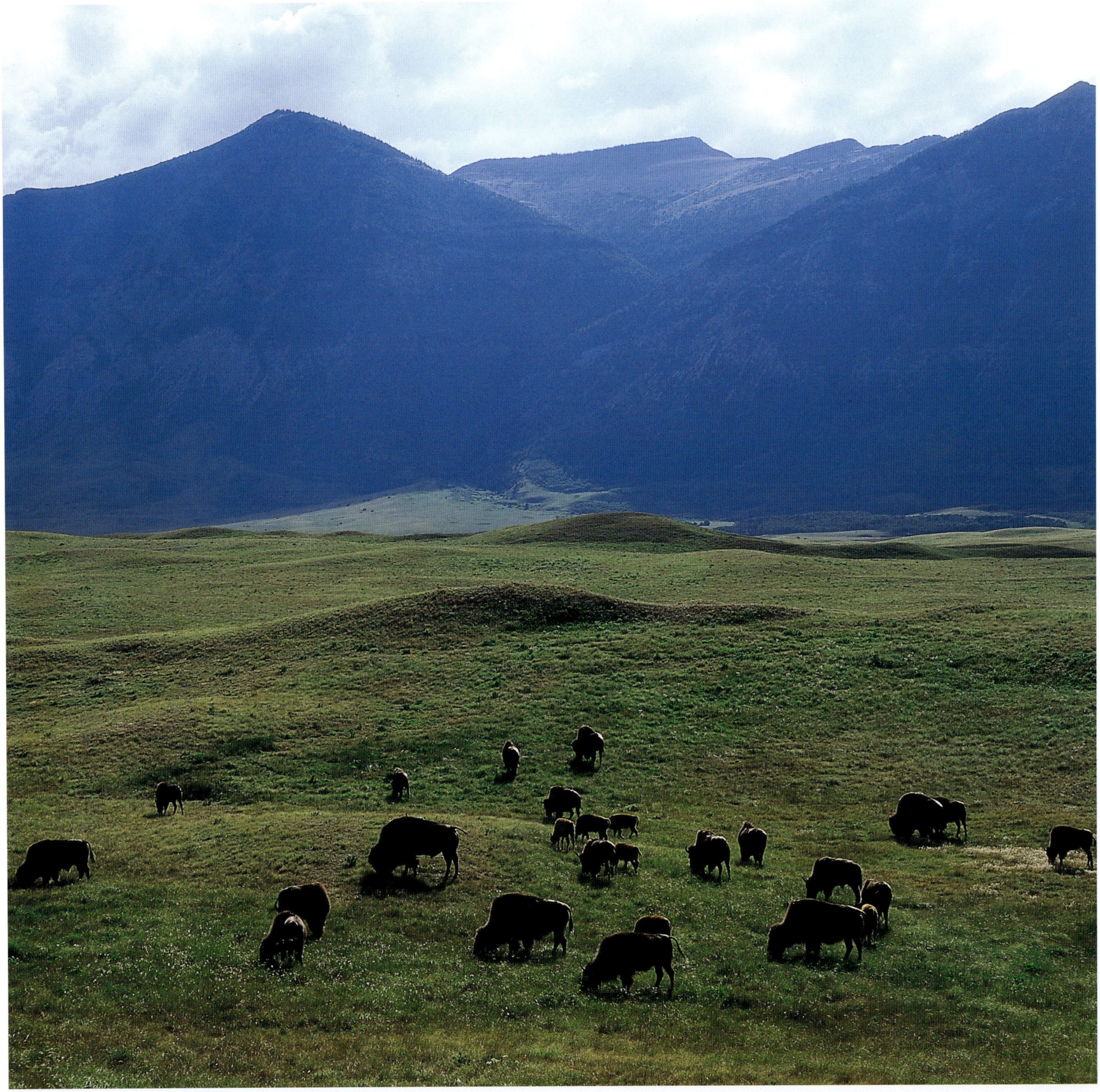

*M*t. Chephren (3266m) dominates the scene over Lower Waterfowl Lake and the Mistaya River – however, Howse Peak (3290m), on the left, is 24m higher and "little" Chephren Lake is nearly 3 km in length. This is a pristine and beautiful ecosystem. Banff National Park.

Left: *A*s the settling of the prairies pushed west, millions of Buffaloes, or Bison (Bison bison) were hunted to near extinction. Today, only a few herds exist in National Parks and private reserves. Here a small paddock, in Waterton Lakes National Park, protects a small but healthy herd – assuring the survival of this great, fascinating beast.

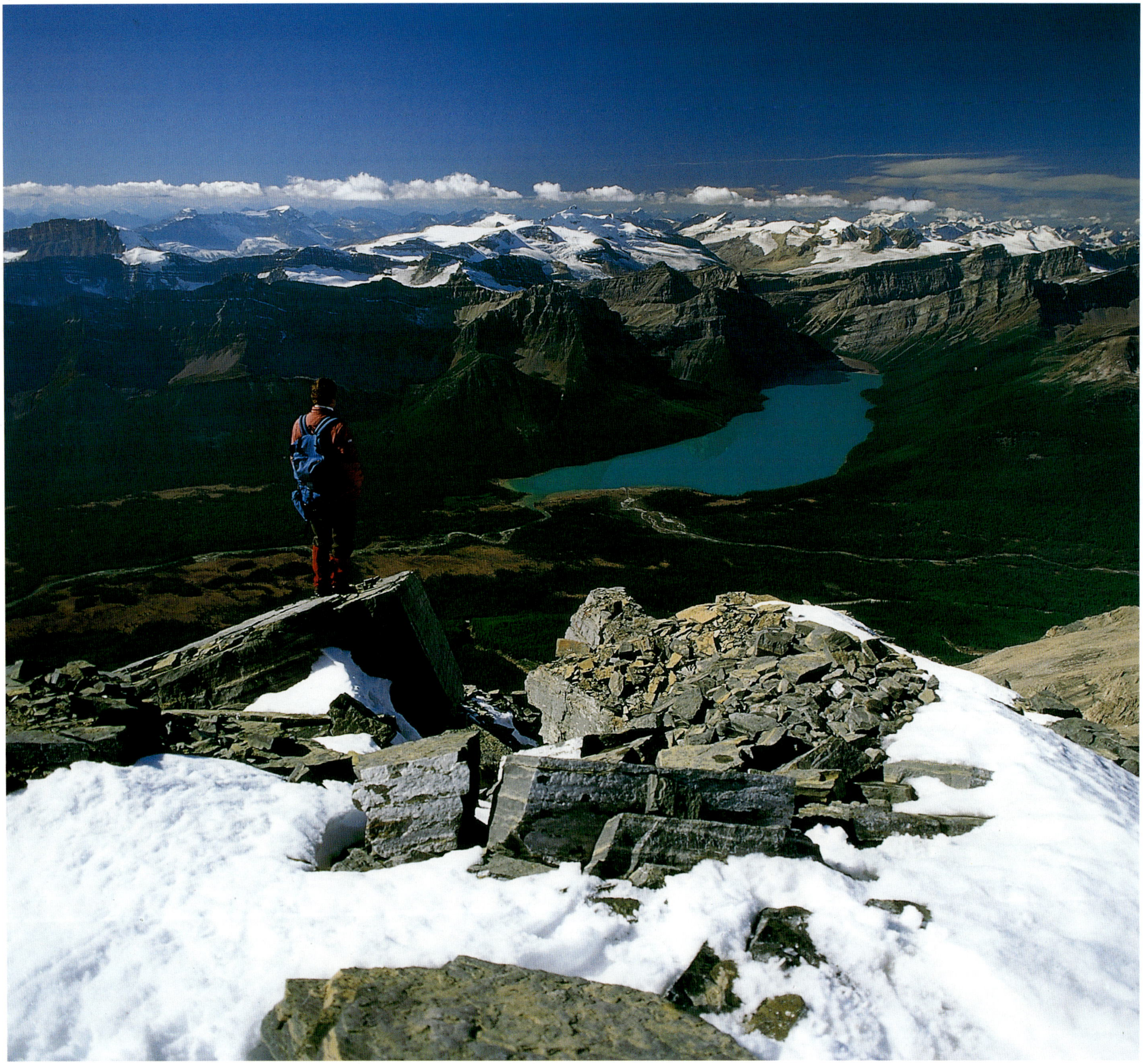

Jasper National Park is, mostly, a true pristine wilderness, full of natural wonders like Maligne Lake. It is accessible by road as far as the lakehead – beyond that lies a vast wilderness that is explored only by hardy hikers via only a few trails. This glacial lake is 22 km long and is flanked on both sides by high mountains, with its apex at the far end, where Mt. Brazeau (3468m) and a large icefield provide most of the glacial blue-green water for the lake. Fishing? The usual – one day they bite, the next they do not.

Left: Mount Hector (3394m) is either close to heaven, or it is heaven – a very beautiful area and great fun to climb. To the west, the turquoise Hector Lake nestles at the foot of the Wapta Icefield, dominated by Mt. Balfour (3272m). First climbed in 1895 by the Abbot-Fay-Thompson team. In those days, people climbed mountains the hard way, and with passion and love, walking here from Lake Louise, camping on the mountain and walking back the next day, a 50 km round trip – with no real trail to follow.

The Third Vermilion Lake settles in a large, marshy area along the Bow River, just west of the town of Banff. Despite a large number of visitors, the site appears to have a healthy ecosystem. The north end of the Sundance Range reflects its snowy peaks as a Black Bird guards its nest. Spring has arrived. Banff National Park.

Ready to face the winter, a family of sheep relaxes near Jasper on a sunny October day. The long, harsh seven-month winter requires incredible endurance from all animals. Many will die from the cold or starvation, or as meals for carnivores. The harsh law of Nature is executed by the fair bush justice, which allows species to continue.

This is the less known east face of Mt. Athabasca (3490m), on the left, as viewed on a winter morning. The lesser peak on the right is 3094m in height and flanks the northern Mt. Athabasca Glacier. Big-time explorers J.N. Collie and H. Wooley first explored it, in 1898. From there, they were the first to see the Columbia Icefield. Banff/Jasper National Parks.

The craggy southeast face of Grotto Mtn (2706m), located northwest of Lac des Arcs, at the south end of the Fairholme Range. Many interesting rock climbing routes lead to the summit - most on the southwest face. One could call it "an ugly pile of rock", and it is, but because of the sunrise's pinkish hues and the clouds and shadows below it, this may be called an interesting or even pretty image.

*S*pring is just around the corner as break-up is in progress on the Mistaya River. A good month more will pass before greenery replaces the snow. Still very wintry, Mt. Chephren (3266m) stands guard, waiting for the long, harsh winter to go away – after all, it is May 15. Banff National Park.

It is called the Prairie Crocus or Pasque Flower (Pulsatilla ludoviciana) yet it grows in the mountains? Actually, it is a true anemone and not related to the Crocus. The flowers do slightly resemble the European Crocus, but the stem and leaves are very different. It can be found by the Foothills and Prairies, along the Mackenzie River to the Arctic Coast.

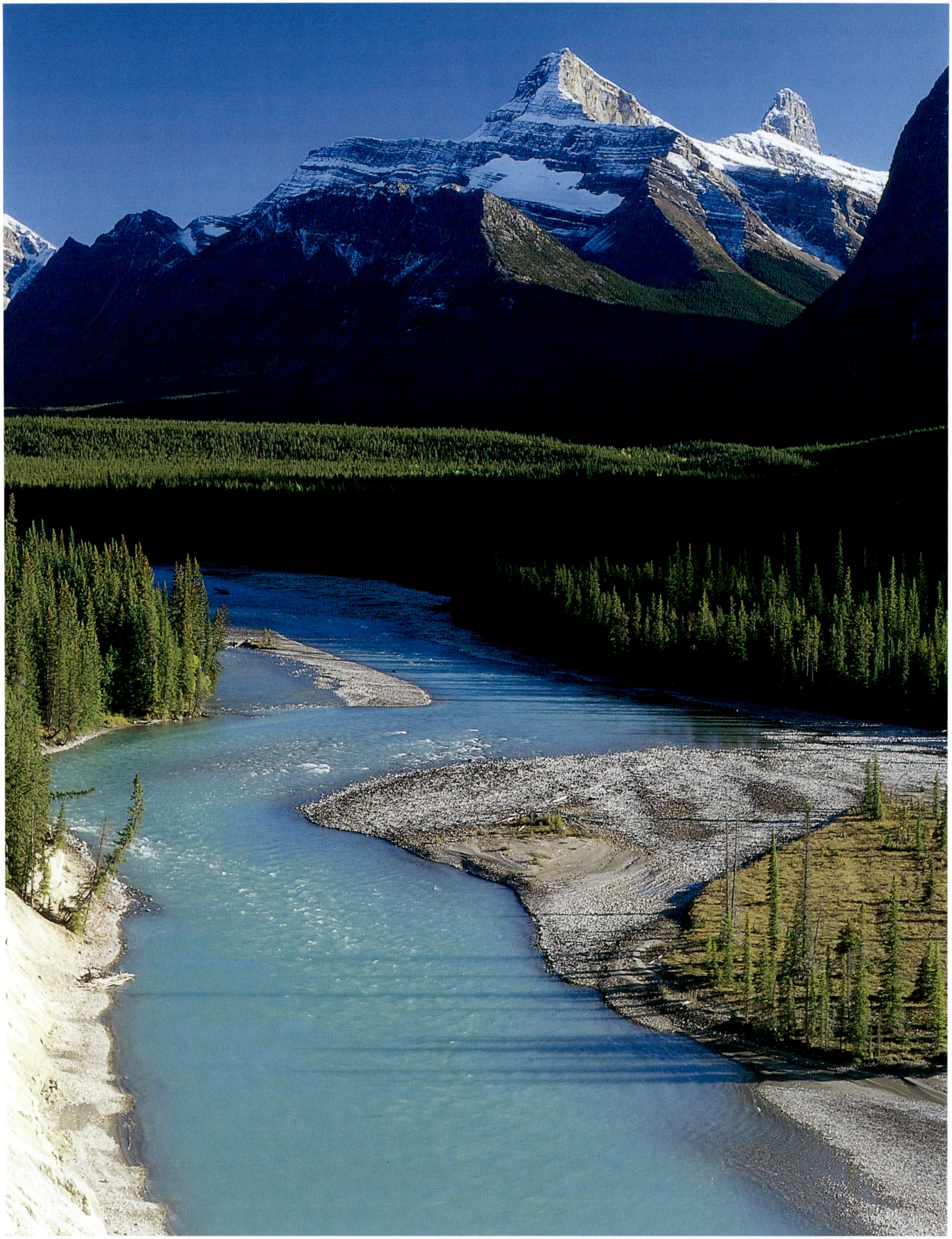

*M*aligne Lake is cool and the Opal Hills, from which the photo was taken, is cooler – literally. The elevation of the lake is 1673m and cold water, coming from glaciers, creates a cold microclimate in the valley. Thus only high-altitude vegetation thrives here and only a few, hardy animals spend the summer here – among them Moose, Mountain Caribou and Grizzly Bears. Jasper National Park.

Left: *O*ne of the great Rocky Mountain rivers, the Athabasca River is born at the foot of Mt. Columbia, by the Columbia Icefield. It flows north to join the mighty Mackenzie and empties into the Arctic Ocean. Mt. Christie (3103m) graces the central background. The white cliffs on the left contain rich mineral deposits and are the feeding grounds for a healthy herd of goats that live on Mt. Kerkeslin, north of here.

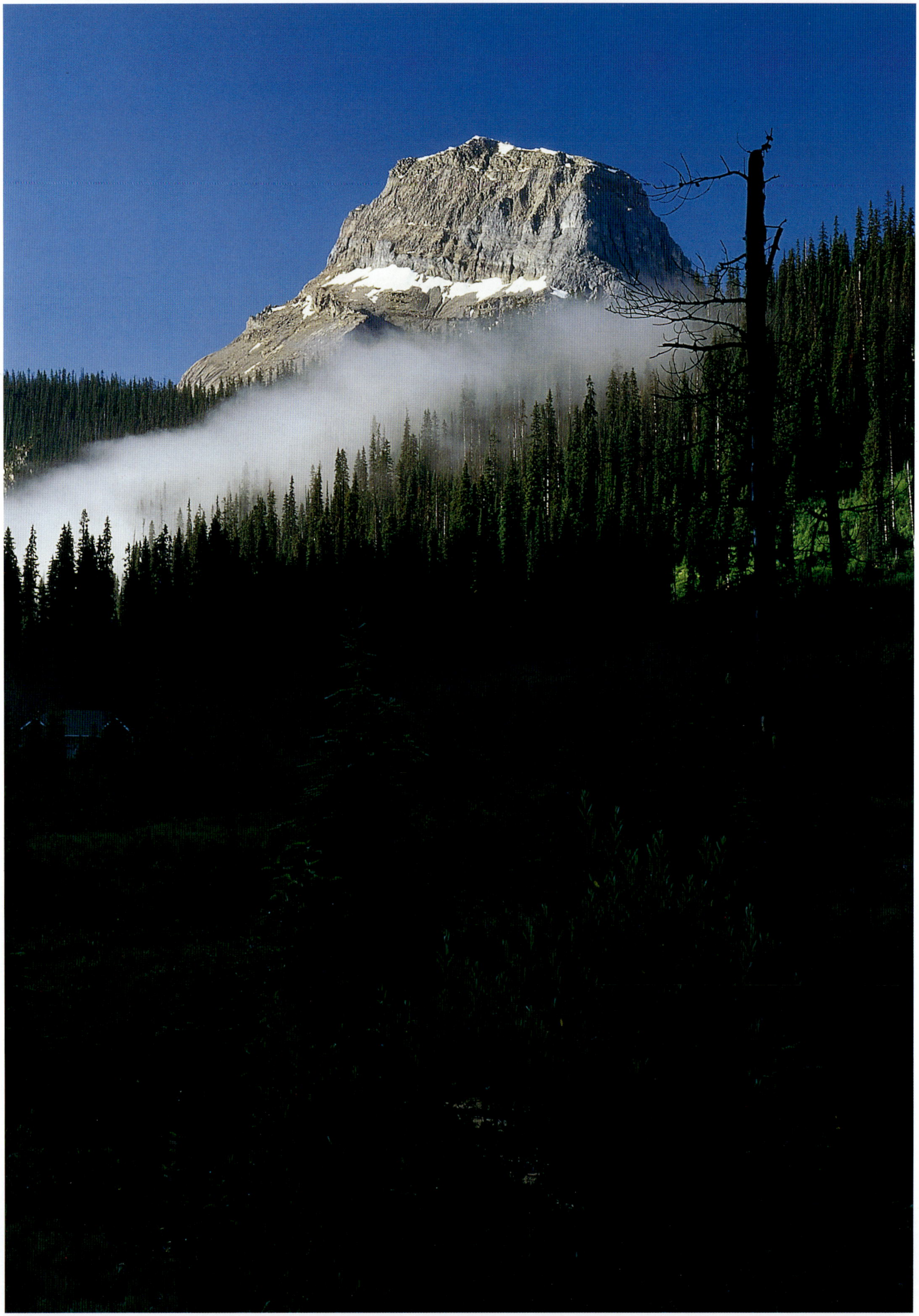

The spider took the time to build its source of livelihood and then the night's dew beautified the web – which, at sunrise, looks like a lovely necklace of pearls. A few minutes later, the sun burned away some of the clouds and Wapta Mountain (2778m) revealed its rocky northeast face (opposite). These photos were taken in the upper part of the Yoho Valley. Yoho National Park is small, but full of magical natural wonders and is well worth visiting.

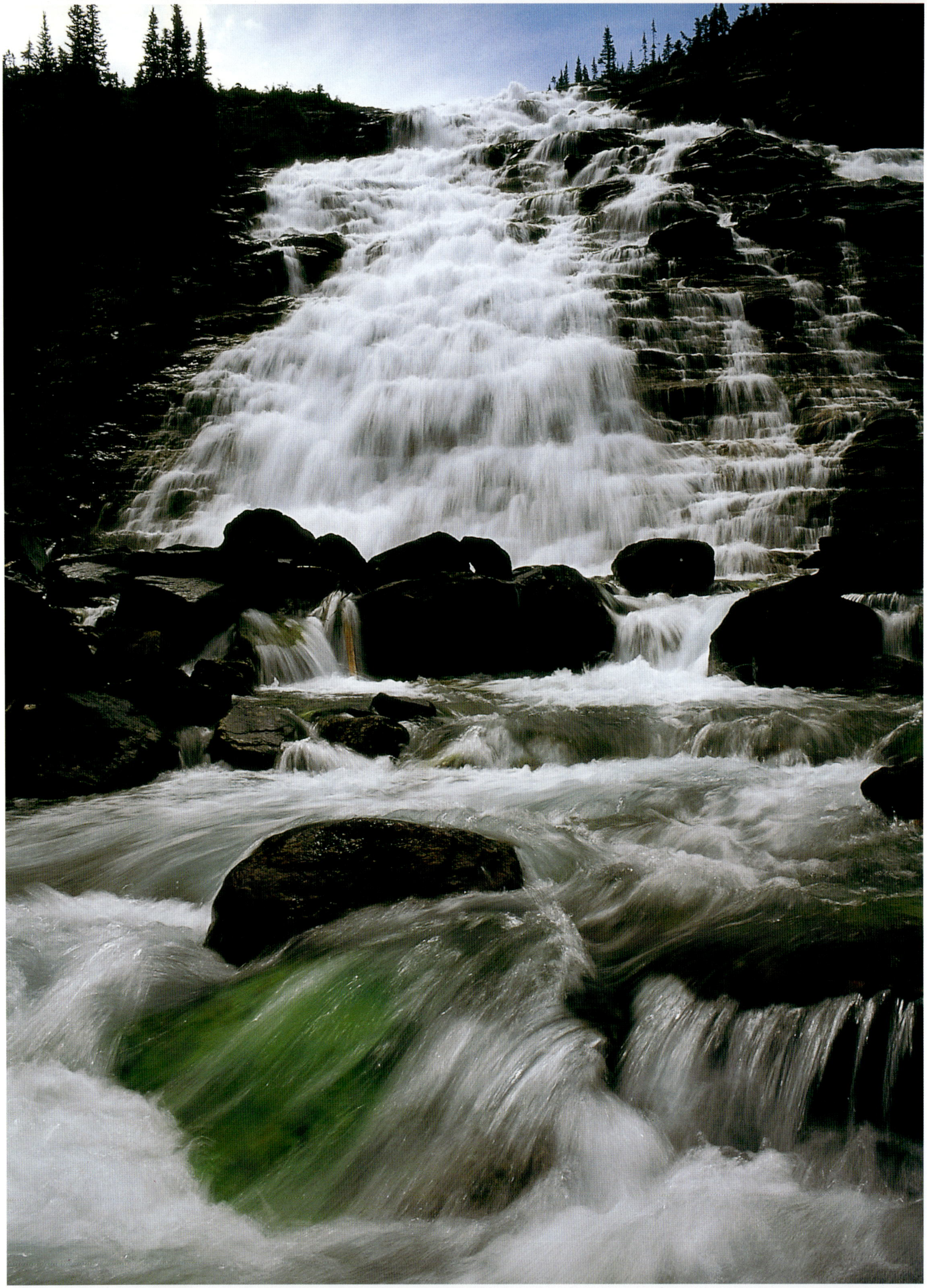

Close-up photography is probably the most interesting and difficult – and therefore rewarding – of all. So much is involved here that time and patience are musts. A sudden wind might shake off the rain droplets; a light breeze might move it, making photography impossible – such close-ups require closing the lens to, say, f22, which may require an exposure of several seconds. The author loves high altitude photography as much as close-up work and could publish an entire book on the subject.

Left: The hidden Geraldine Valley, in Jasper National Park, is blessed with several large lakes and waterfalls. Early summer is the best time to see the roaring whitewaters, while August presents a wide variety of flowers. Wildlife common to the valley includes Grizzly Bears, Goats, Wolves and the occasional Mountain Caribou. An interesting loop, from the upper valley, east to Fryatt Valley, could be made in two or three days. The area has a lot to offer and provides accommodation in campgrounds and the Fryatt Hut.

Bivouacking on the summit of Mt. Alderson (2692m), in Waterton Lakes National Park, allowed for this bronzed in the rising sun photo. The view is to the south and encompasses, mostly, the Montana Rockies – only 3 km away. The massive Mt. Cleveland dominates the left horizon. It was here that a nasty Packrat nearly ate the author alive – see the story, Leo the Packrat.

When bivouacking on a mountain, one's gear often gets soggy – or just plain wet. If the next day is sunny and warm, all will dry quickly. If the next day is rainy, then mountaineering is not so much fun. Here the author dries his stuff on the lower slopes of Mt. Clitheroe, in front of the fascinating The Ramparts, in the Tonquin Valley. Jasper National Park.

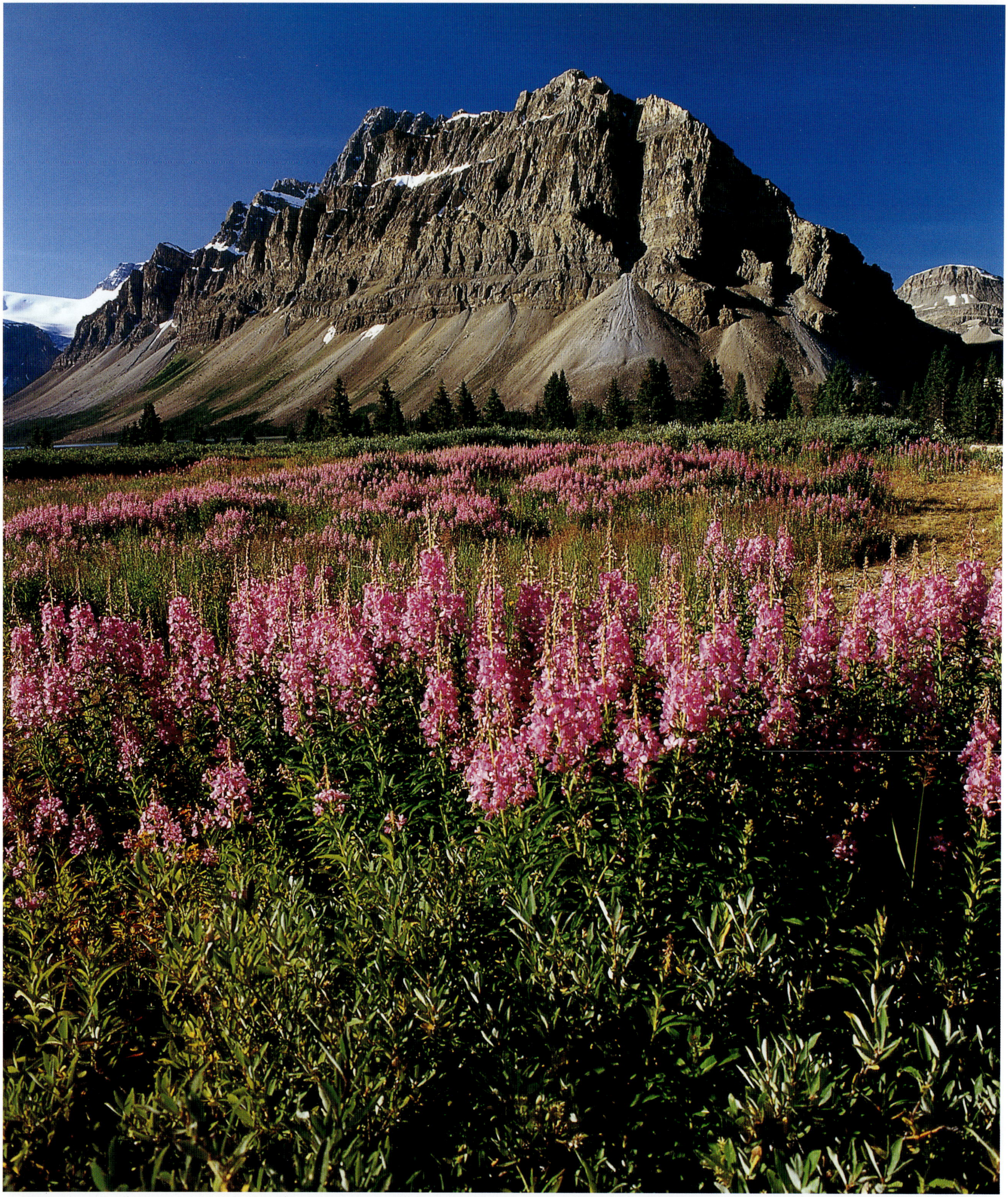

A great big, friendly spruce tree trunk shares space with a host of plants and flowers. The showy Indian Paintbrush (Castilleja miniata) finds very fertile soil here, allowing it to grow to near its maximum height, 30 cm. Kootenay National Park.

Left: By the turquoise Bow Lake, where nature is rich and lush, fields of Fireweed (Epilobium angustifolium) can be enjoyed in mid-August. Crowfoot Mountain (3050m) and the deep blue Alberta skies complement this peaceful summer's day photo. Banff National Park.

Beautiful But Dangerous

The fascinating, lofty and challenging Rockies are like a magnet – luring people to their heights year round. For people from the plains, they are a real "terra incognita" just waiting to be discovered. Little do they realize that the mountains are also "terra dangerous". Tragic accidents can happen here at any time. Avalanches of snow, ice and rock are killers; falling from a steep cliff or slipping into whitewater rapids can be fatal; encounters with wild animals can be trouble; freezing temperatures, hypothermia or falling into crevasses often end in tragedy. A very common problem is getting lost in the woods. As a result, going deep into the mountains, solo, must be strongly discouraged.

In most of the above cases, quick, efficient help can save lives – but only if there are people around to give that help. The best way to be safe in the mountains is to travel in groups of three or more. In our individualistic society, while people may start their journey in a group, along the way they often split into smaller groups, or go solo. "I don't want to go any further." "I want to go back." "I want to go this way," I want ...

"I" is often the reason for serious accidents. How? In a maze of trails, if one hiker turns left and another turns right, they will soon lose track of each other. One might be carrying such equipment as a tent, a stove and food, while the other will have to do without. One might break an arm or a leg and the other won't be there to help.

Bears, cougars and wolves can tell when someone is injured and they will attack. So? Never, ever separate. Stay together in a group. When one must stop, all must stop. The best and most civilized way to hike is to put the weakest member of the group at the front, with the leader going last to make sure that no one is left behind. Never leave anyone behind on the assumption that they will catch up. What if he takes a wrong turn or is confronted by a dangerous animal? Again, these are good possibilities for tragedy.

A couple went for a scramble up a medium-sized mountain. Three-quarters of the way up, the lady got tired, so the man went for the summit solo while she waited. The cold, wind and boredom forced her down the slopes. She went left instead of right and wound up by some dangerous cliffs a kilometer from the trail.

When the man came down from the summit, he couldn't find her and assumed she had gone down to the car. When he got to the parking lot, she wasn't there so he figured she had hitched a ride to their hotel. He didn't find her at the hotel, so he asked the police for help. The next morning, at daybreak, a search was launched and, after six hours of intensive searching, she was found nearly dead of exposure from the cold September night at the top of a rugged cliff – unable to go up or down and in a state of severe mental breakdown.

Two women and four teenagers went for an overnight trip to a mountain hut. As usual, the kids ran along the trail, getting ahead of their mothers and separating from the group. The kids thought that their mothers would catch up and kept rushing forward. In their hurry, the kids took a wrong turn and, not knowing the area, wound up in unfamiliar territory without food, warm clothing or adequate shelter for the cold mountain night.

In the meantime, one of the mothers had sprained her ankle and could not continue, so the two ladies returned to their car hoping the kids would be allright at the hut. The next day, hikers coming down from the hut informed the mothers that they hadn't seen any kids there and a search was launched.

Because the kids had taken a wrong turn, it complicated the search, making things very difficult for the rescue party. By sheer accident, two passing hikers found the kids - dehydrated, hypothermic, very hungry and unable to walk because of blisters on their feet. The four were extremely lucky that they hadn't encountered a Grizzly Bear overnight. Rescuers, directed by the two hikers, found the kids near evening and got them back to their mothers before midnight. They had survived by huddling together under a tree in the freezing temperatures.

Four climbers set out to climb a mountain via glaciated slopes. They were experienced climbers, roped together and properly equipped. As often happens, a large expanse of snow covered ice seemed safe and prompted them to unrope and they made it safely to the summit. After a bit of exploration, it came time to return. The leader, with the rope coiled around his neck, went first followed by one of the other three. The remaining two followed slowly and, in the rolling icefield landscape, they lost visual contact and got separated. The two climbers in the lead figured the others would catch up and returned to the road. The two slower climbers stopped for a breather and a snack. Soon afterward, one broke through a thin snow bridge and fell into a deep crevasse. His friend panicked when he could not make visual or verbal contact with him. With no rope, or any rescue equipment, the friend ran down to get help. The first two climbers were gone... to get a beer.

By the time rescuers were ready to move out, it was nightfall. The search began immediately and, in extremely adverse conditions, rescuers located the crevasse by following footprints in the snow. After two hours of cutting ice in the crevasse, they brought up the body of the young climber.

On this trip, whatever could go wrong did go wrong. On a glacier, you never, ever unrope and separate. What a tragic waste of a young life. What a senseless tragedy. What irresponsible behaviour.

Many times, similar situations occur - people split up, leaving their partners at the mercy of the wilderness. This is a common and disturbing problem – even with climbing clubs, which are mandated to provide safe and enjoyable mountaineering.

Clearly, more effort is required to rethink and improve both the education and ethics of the mountaineering culture.

Following simple, common sense rules and maintaining discipline could have easily prevented all the above-mentioned accidents. Discipline? What's that? Many people today have no conception of that noun. Rugged individualism can lead you to a rugged end. In the mountains or the woods, always stay with the group – never, ever separate – it just might save your life. And you will enjoy your trip more fully. Factoid : majority of mountain accidents happen when crossing creeks or fording rivers.

Still on the subject of mountain safety, the author would like to pay homage and last respects to a remarkable climber, guide and beautiful human being. Carl Conrad Nagy who died, tragically, on Mt. Little in August of 2000, just 3km from where the author climbed the Tower of Babel.

The Dangers of Mountains

Some people climb mountains for many years and are lucky enough to escape with only a few scrapes and bruises. Is it knowledge, destiny or luck?

I was one of those who spent most of my life climbing without a hitch. Sometimes, I proclaimed that I felt safer climbing a mountain - where my safety was mostly up to me - than on city streets full of crooks who might cause a great deal of trouble.

Once I had a brush with danger when I fell off a wall and injured my back, and on another occasion, a large rock fell on my foot and cracked a bone. Both times I got off lightly. As a result, the older I grew, the more blasé about danger I became. I took things lightly and got away with it for a long time.

Recently, I went for a little walkabout - looking for flowers, or a marmot to photograph. I discovered a small waterfall, about 5 meters high, with lush greenery surrounding it - a pretty photo to be taken, I thought. I started working on it - a few images taken before I found another great angle. It required climbing a steep little cliff and it gave a much better perspective.

It was a clear, crisp morning - ideal conditions for good photography. The only thing that was not ideal was the cliff's face - it was rotten and wet. I am not sure how it happened, but I just fell off, rolling head over heels until I landed in that photogenic creek. When I regained consciousness, I was lying face down in the water. As I evaluated my predicament, I realized that I was only a short distance from the top of the falls and drifting down. Somehow, in record time, I got to dry land.

That same summer, in Kananaskis, an experienced hiker was crossing a creek over a wet log when he slipped down, hit his head on the rocks, lost consciousness and drowned.

In a split second, I had a supernatural, out-of-life experience. I actually saw that Kananaskis accident clearly - which probably helped me get out of the creek so quickly.

Wet and unhappy, I decided to go to my car and change clothes, since the morning was fairly chilly. When I tried to take up my backpack, I felt a very strange sensation - I could not lift it. Then I noticed that my yellow sweater was more red than yellow. Blood was pouring over my face and I couldn't figure out from where. Since the road was only 2 kilometers away, I decided to rush down before I bled to death.

For a moment, I wanted to stop and take a photograph of my gory condition, but the flowing blood told me to move quickly, or else! Then I noticed that my right hand was hanging down in a strange way and I realized that both bones above my wrist were broken. Yet I did not feel a thing - nothing at all.

Rushing down to the road, I realized that I was leaving a trail of blood - something that might attract the attention of a bear's keen nose.

Fortunately, I soon stumbled across three people hiking up the trail. They casually asked, as they came along, "Are you alright?" I politely responded, "No I am not." Later, I thought they must have hearts of stone - but since I looked like I had been attacked by a grizzly, which could mean problems for them - they carried on up the slope, unconcerned.

When I reached the highway, I encountered a tour bus and its horrified driver called for an ambulance. Two hours later, I had my head sewn up by... medical students (ouch!) and my hand repaired by a doctor who specialized in broken bones.

When I was discharged, the doctor told me, "I did what I could but there may still be a bone out of place, so go to your doctor and hospital and check it out."

I was wobbly, from loss of blood - obviously traumatized, when the nurse announced, "You are all done. Ready to go." It was near evening, I was in a strange place far from home and was covered in blood. This was none of the nurse's concern. Finally, because I insisted, she allowed me to use a public restroom to clean away the blood.

As I was leaving, I encountered a paramedic who took really good care of me in his ambulance. He insisted that I was not well enough to be going anywhere and arranged it so I could have emergency overnight accommodation for $35 - instead of $300 for a night in the hospital. (I always thought we had free medical care here...) I also had to pay for most of the ambulance costs. Still, this exceptional young paramedic went out of his way to help me. He even brought me a sandwich and some juice, and checked me out. He, and not a hospital employee, woke me up the next morning and tied my shoelaces (which I could not do for myself) before taking me to a cafeteria and arranging a free ride in a tour bus so that I could pick up my car - which I had left along the highway. I would like to thank this beautiful human being and the bus people as well.

As the emergency doctor told me, I went to my local hospital to have my wrist checked. I did, indeed, require another operation to fix what he had not done right.

After the second operation, as I was resting in the recovery room, acute pain set in. I was tied to an intravenous system and unable to move freely. Two hours passed with no one checking in on me, although I heard some young nurses giggling at a nearby station. I called out and one came to see me. When I asked for a pain-killing pill, she told me that she could only give me a needle. I proclaimed that I had had enough needles over the last two days. She and the other nurses laughed out loud and said, "See how quickly he passes on the needle!" And they left.

Soon afterward, a more mature nurse came by and she promptly brought me a pill she took from a cabinet directly above those lazy nurses to whom a patient's pain was a joke!

It was my first time in a hospital and I had no idea how to deal with broken bones. Nobody told me anything; they were in such a rush. "Go home," they said, "Come back in 6 weeks." Too late, I found out that my arm, which was in a cast, should have been exercised to prevent the muscles, tendons and veins from atrophying and cutting into blood circulation. Intensive physiotherapy and my own efforts did much less than expected. Now, two years after I broke it, my right hand is functioning at only 50% and, being a very active middle-aged man, I am more or less disabled.

If we allow doctors and nurses like those I encountered, to practice – we will have many more disabled people around who could otherwise be productive. Even so, the thing that hurt me most during my second operation and recovery time in the hospital, was that no one ever looked at me, or smiled at me. No one put a hand on my shoulder and said, "you will be alright." The long-faced hospital staff acted like robots.

Another upsetting feature of a hospital is its parking. Meters are set for such a short duration that by the time you check in and see a doctor, a big ticket is hanging on your windshield. Traumatized, injured, nearly dead people come to a hospital for help and a heartless penny collector lurks nearby to punish them with tickets, or by having their cars towed away. It is cruel to pick on the sick and helpless. Hospitals, and especially emergency wards, should have convenient, free or very low-priced parking with friendly, helpful attendants – not like the one I encountered. "Move or I will have you towed away now," he barked.

Recently, the World Health Organization ranked Canada's healthcare system 30th in the world – in contradiction of our beloved politicians' claims that we are the world's best – in everything.

Still on the subject of broken bones, a wise old story comes to mind: Two friends were hiking in the woods when, suddenly, a bear surprised them. One, who was more fit, climbed into a tree. The other was attacked and knocked down – the bear mauled him for awhile and left. The first fellow climbed down from the tree and asked his injured friend, "Why did that bear huff and puff over you for so long?" His friend replied, "The bear shared some of his wisdom with me: "We find out who our true friends are when we are in trouble."

After I broke my arm, I found out how few good friends I really had. I discontinued most those "friendships" at once. Of what use is a friend who is not there when you need him?

Regardless of these sad and somber, but admittedly educational experiences – which I do appreciate, my life continued on and I did not spend much time whining or feeling sorry for myself. Five days after the accident, I was back in the mountains – taking photos of the gorgeous flowers, I was doing what I love the most... with one hand. My only regret is that I lost a season of mountaineering – but I still hiked a lot and took many lovely photos, a number of them are featured in this volume.

The Global Outlook

As advancing technology makes the world seem smaller, everything, including the environment must be viewed from a global perspective. There are countries that protect their own ecology while importing vast quantities of, say, timber from other countries – knowing all too well that trees are the only true and efficient air purifier and that forests are the very essence of a healthy, functioning ecology. However, only large forests can perform that function successfully.

One large tree can absorb and neutralize about 5 kilograms of carbon monoxide a year. One hectare of forest will produce 6 tons of pure oxygen per year. Small forests located near major sources of pollution cannot cope and will sicken and die. Even larger forests will eventually sicken and die. Only extremely large forests, with more than enough trees to cope with pollution, can hope to survive.

There are three main sources of pollution that endanger our forests and ourselves: local - within 100 km, regional - within 300 - 500 km and global - mostly falling from the sky in the form of acid rain.

While the first two are controllable, the third is not. Any pollution, anywhere in the world, contributes to global pollution, in the same way that any green space contributes to a global fresh air bank.

When one lives in Alaska, Northern Canada, Scandinavia, Siberia, Brazil or Australia, one is mostly affected by global pollution and life is still healthy and wholesome. If one lives in heavily populated and industrialized places like Mexico City, Tokyo, New York, Chicago, Shanghai, Ruhr, or the Silesian Industrial District, one has little chance to live a long, healthy life – many in these areas die long before retirement.

In many countries, huge industrial complexes are built next to priceless ancient cities or even more priceless wilderness and soon both are destroyed in the name of progress.

Priceless historical sites, like the Roman Coliseum and the Greek Acropolis, are crumbling under the pressures of large, noisy, polluted cities. Mexico City is located on a high plateau, which has no rivers or lakes, and 20 million people have to rely on underground water. As the water is pumped out at an enormous rate, the structure of the very land itself collapses and many buildings are ruined and lives lost. A city with no reliable source of water may become a ghost town at any time, should earthquakes and drought hit at the same time.

The rapidly growing cities of Phoenix and Tucson, Arizona also have very little in the way of water supply. All their green gardens, lawns and golf courses are kept on the equivalent of a respirator, using up valuable water. If global warming increases even a little faster than expected, the Colorado River will not be able to provide enough *drinking* water for Arizona – let alone golf courses and green lawns. The desert will quickly reclaim that artificial oasis. The same fate could await the Salt Lake City area, where the cities grow as their water supply decreases.

As the global population grows, deforestation follows and desert expansion is a likely consequence. Fifty years ago, the island of Madagascar was covered in lush forests – home of some of the rarest plants – plants that were the source of many "miracle cures". Since then, as the island's population exploded, the forest has receded until there is a thin strip left along the east coast. People there cut the trees down to cook their meals. The same disaster has happened in much of Africa – trees were cut down and the desert expanded.

Large forests can effectively resist desert expansion, but small woodlands will be swallowed up. What will happen when Brazil has eliminated the majority of its Amazon Rainforest? Most likely a small part of the jungle will survive as forest, but the high plateaus to the south will become semi-desert as they are deprived of moisture from the jungle. What is Brazil aiming for? Becoming richer and stronger? Deforestation will lead to large areas of desert and then poverty and devastation to the world's ecology.

There are those who believe that planting a forest of billions of trees east of Alice Springs, in Australia's Simpson Desert, would produce and keep enough moisture in the area to change Australia from a nation of mostly desert to a lush green paradise. A large pipeline would be needed to bring desalinated seawater from the coast to get the process started - a fine "pet project" for someone who has a spare $10 billion.

Similar projects have been successful in the former Soviet Union. Temperate deserts in Kazakstan suffered strong winds, which blew away the sandy soil. Huge belts of trees were planted, which stopped the winds, brought in moisture and allowed agriculture to prosper there.

What is happening to Australia's Koala Bear? These lovely creatures rely upon the eucalyptus tree for food (as Panda Bears rely upon bamboo shoots). As Australia's economy grows, eucalyptus trees are cut down in ever increasing numbers to make room for new developments - leaving the Koala to die. It seems that no one cares.

The destruction of wildlife habitats is the major reason for wildlife destruction. Like homeless people, wildlife with no home base is doomed.

How do badly planned industries affect a country and its people? Let's look at Germany's Ruhr, Saar and Westphalia Districts. There we see huge concentrations of coal mines, smelters, coke plants and all sorts of manufacturing located in a very small area. Over 10 million people live in these areas, in substandard conditions and with hardly any air to breathe. The Rhine River, once the pride of Europe, is now a very polluted, poisoning the North Sea. Bad planning equals bad consequences.

Similarly, the coalfields and heavy industry of Moravia and Silesia poison The Czech Republic, Slovakia and Poland. The Oder and Vistula Rivers empty their polluted waters into the Baltic Sea - destroying its marine life. Ironically, all these industries are also located by the foothills of the Carpathian Mountains, where the rivers provide drinking water for about 20 million people.

Instead of cleaning up this polluted area, which is barely fit for human habitation, large cities and more industries are being built right in the mountains. Instead of creating large National Parks to protect the already half-dead Tatra and Carpathian Mountains, they are destroying them completely.

Because of their sheer size and motion, our oceans may be sickly, but they are still alive. Small inland seas, surrounded by heavy population and industry, are nearly dead. The Black, Caspian and Baltic Seas are now reservoirs of toxic pollutants and all life in them will cease to exist in the next few decades. The polluted water of the Rhine and Thames Rivers are just about to meet halfway, to create a new "Black Sea" where the North Sea is now.

It is a very scary thing to think about what China's exploding industries will do to the world's ecology. Within 25 years, China's population will exceed 2 billion and Shanghai alone, will be home to 30 million souls while the Yangtze River will become a central industrial canal. By that time, Japan will run out of tropical islands from which to clear-cut logs and will be well on the way to cutting down Siberian forests.

World industry desperately needs a lot of pulp, paper and cardboard. I've said it before and I'll say it again: buy cereal, cookies, chips, et cetera, and you will get a large box with a plastic bag inside that is less than half the size of the box. So half of the cardboard is just wasted. 50% more trees are cut down to continue this senseless waste. Is anyone listening? Is anyone thinking? Does anyone care?

One wonders why we have Governments if they don't help in these important areas. They could force industry to produce a full container, whether it's a box of cereal or anything else. Why wouldn't a Government do that? By stopping the waste of 50% more trees, we would cut pollution and that means costs would go down. Since pulp plants are among the most ecologically harmful, requiring great amounts of water and energy, while releasing great quantities of toxic pollutants into the air, water and soil.

The more paper we use, the more pollution we cause. So please use paper wisely and recycle.

Now, let's talk about the 43,000 people in Canada, and 4 million worldwide, who die every year from smoking tobacco.

Statistics show that tobacco kills three times more people than AIDS, drugs, alcohol, murders, suicides and car accidents *combined*. Now think about this: all these people not only kill themselves voluntarily, they pay as much as $180,000 for the privilege! For the same money, you could buy a nice home, get a really good education, buy a dozen cars or plant thousands of trees to green up your city. You could even take fifty nice vacations or just eat really well for many years and have a long, healthy life. Instead, many people elect to ruin their health and die early.

We still have no law that actually prohibits children from smoking and statistics show that 30% of smokers begin before the age of 13; 85% of them begin before they are 16.

Lung cancer now kills more women than breast cancer. Since one of eight women gets breast cancer, if something doesn't change, soon there will be very few women around. Aside from its more deadly aspects, smoking destroys facial skin - a women who smokes will certainly look like a fifty-year-old prostitute when she's thirty.

In civilized countries, the law prohibits smoking before the age of 18, or 19, and is strictly enforced. Here, in this "free country", a law like that would be unenforceable, so we simply don't have that law.

Each year, billions of dollars go up in smoke - lost to forest fires, house and business fires as well as the injuries and deaths that occur as a result. All because of careless, senseless smoking. And then, we do not have the money to fund adequate healthcare and education.

Tobacco is a big killer, but it is only the tip of the iceberg. What about alcoholism and the common use of illegal drugs? These things destroy lives too. So what if some drugs are illegal? It's a free country - we can do what we want, or so say many people.

Judging by all these attitudes, one wonders what the world's societies and ecology will be like in 50 years. Will everything be legal, including law breaking?, will presecuting criminals be unconstitutional?

National Parks: The Global Issue

If you have ever visited a National Park, you will have realized that it is a very special place: a Cathedral of Nature; a museum of the past and the present; a place for learning and admiration. In our rapidly changing, or rather deteriorating world ecology, we are reminded that National Parks are not just lovely places to visit, but areas necessary to maintain the quality of the very air we breathe and water we drink.

In a time when bulldozers and chainsaws outnumber people with common sense and wisdom, things have gotten too far out of hand too quickly. The world ecology is in an awful mess. The rapid growth of population and industry, our production and consumption, directly correlate to increase of garbage and industrial waste - which is causing global pollution. Without a major, worldwide effort to curb this growth, our planet will be damaged beyond repair much sooner than most people think.

It is only 50 years since the real industrial era began and what a mess it has made of our planet. Imagine what it will be like in 100 years when everything is doubling about every 30 years.

Look at what the Mexicans have done for "progress". Sierra Madre Occidental, once green and full of life, is now a pitiful sight - nearly all the virgin forests are gone and with them, the Grizzly Bear, Wolf, the Imperial Woodpecker (the world's largest) and scores of other species.

In 1936, Australia declared the Tasmanian Tiger an endangered species but, endangered or not, hunters finally shot them all. In that same year, the Tiger became extinct.

Brazil continues to destroy the Amazon Jungle at the rate of over 30,000 square kilometers per year in search of *riches* and *progress*. Does the "Affluenza" bug infect the whole world? Do people still think that more is better?

Tampering with nature destroys the balance of nature; drastically changes the climate; causes floods in dry areas and drought in wet areas: spawning hurricanes, tornadoes and tsunamis in stable regions. The dry Australia and North Sahara get wetter, while the humid Central Europe gets drier and warmer. West Africa, Chile and Japan are becoming much drier, while Eastern Canada becomes more humid. The Canadian Arctic is becoming warmer at an alarming rate - which may cause the Arctic ice to melt more rapidly and prevent the Gulf Stream from moving into the North. This would leave Iceland, Scandinavia and Northern Russia icebound.

Man's tampering with nature is causing these things. The hole in the ozone layer over Antarctica is larger than ever, because of ozone-destroying chlorofluorocarbons. Now a hole is growing over the North Pole as well.

Why not protect the things that protect us from extinction - the forests of the world? It is useless to ask timber companies to slow or halt their destruction of our major source of oxygen. Their business is the death of trees.

For change to happen it must come from *all* of us. We must yell as loudly as we can at our governments: "We must protect our forests *now*! Creating small regional parks, where rowdies can drive their dune buggies, four-wheel drives and mountain bikes will only add pollution and destroy the area. WE NEED MANY MORE LARGE NATIONAL PARKS, where the standards of protection are the highest.

We must rethink and re-examine all of our criteria and concepts for National Parks. These parks don't have to be scenic, tourist attractions. As long as it has rivers and lakes, trees and rich flora and fauna, an area is worth protecting.

National Parks, in order to fulfill their mandate to protect nature, must be 1000, or preferably, 2000 square kilometers in area. One bear requires 50-60 sq. km of living space. An eagle requires much, much more. All ungulates - browsers - travel great distances searching for adequate forage. If a park is too small, animals wander outside and get shot, or run over by cars. A large park creates a local microclimate - the proper environment for the local flora and fauna. At present, wild areas are very fragmented - divided by human habitation - that the free movement of wildlife is prevented. This results in inbreeding, which produces an inferior species.

On a related subject, look at what the city of New York has done to salvage its water supply. Since cleaning the seriously polluted Hudson River would be too expensive, the city purchased nearly an entire river's watershed and made any pollution in the area illegal. It was cheaper and will protect a large tract of land that provides clean drinking water and fresh air for the Big Apple. New York's creation of a kind of National Park environment is an example worthy of following.

The worldwide distribution of National Parks is reliant upon each country's wisdom, wealth and natural features. Brazil, the world leader in deforestation, was mostly forest not long ago, so the concept of National Parks was unknown to them - or not necessary. Indonesia, which is second in deforestation, has set aside only 10% of the country for the preservation of natural areas. Large countries like India, Afghanistan, Pakistan and Myanmar have less than 1% of their lands set aside as National Parks. Meanwhile, tiny Nepal discovered the value of such areas and has more National Parks than the four larger countries *combined*! Mexico, which is 14 times larger than Nepal, has barely the same number of such parks.

Europe, affluent but overpopulated and environmentally devastated, struggles with serious pollution of air, water and soil. Some efforts have been made to reverse the catastrophe, but it's too little, too late. Britannia leads the way in Europe. Wales has designated one-third of its land for National Parks and England has followed close behind. Scotland is a distant third, as Ulster has little land protected. Poor Ireland has microscopic National Parks, but with its current wealth, perhaps the wise Irish will be prompted to even out this imbalance.

Italy and Spain protect sumptuous areas of land, but the affluent France does much less. Germany is in a peculiar ecological situation. The country could have a healthy ecology but all the industry is in the northwest and winds carry their pollution all over the country and into their neighbouring countries to the southeast. If the Germans are serious about creating a healthy environment, perhaps they could try to decrease their population growth a bit, buy up land surrounding their existing green areas and return it to its original, natural state. This would require about 20% of Germany's area to compensate for the industrial pollution the country produces. It would be nice if they had fresh air to breathe and pure, fresh water to drink. While it is great to have a high standard of living, it does come with a high price tag. The quality of life decreases drastically in a greatly overpopulated, polluted country. Recht?

Eastern Europe is also a big mess. The communists industrialized the area with absolutely no regard for the environment. Most Eastern European countries have less than 1% of their land protected by park status. Some Parks are as small as 10 sq. km - one wonders what *that* protects... While there is some movement toward clean up and greening the area, it involves very little land and moves at a snail's pace. In the meantime, Eastern European forests and other natural areas are dying. In the Czech Republic, Slovakia and Poland nearly 90% of the forested areas are very sick and will eventually die - will those nations die with them?

Both Canada and the U.S.A. could easily enlarge their National Parks by 50%, considering the size and wealth of these nations and the pollution they create. Australia has 500 National Parks, but mostly, they are too small thus not of much value. Bolivia, which is hardly wealthy, recently established the huge 16,000 sq. km Madidi National Park and is going into ecotourism in a big way - as has Costa Rica. Bravo! South Africa's 23,000 sq. km Kruger National Park generates a huge amount of revenue - as do all the world renowned East African National Parks.

Rumour has it that the Japanese never cut down a tree without planting another two. But it is no rumour that the Japanese use a humungous amount of timber cut down in other parts of the world. Is this wise? Not particularly, since we face great global pollution - like the acid rain that falls worldwide. You cannot get away from it. And as far as those that think that they can protect themselves from pollution by building factories far away from their countries - it just is not so!

Production means pollution. Therefore, do not build more air-poisoning factories. If you have money to invest, invest in the health of the world - buy large tracts of land and plant trees. You will feel great when you leave a green legacy to benefit everyone. Your humble author is as poor as a church mouse, but he has planted 2000 trees to date and plans to plant even more.

A world community, like the United Nations, can impose embargoes and economic sanctions on any country that doesn't want to dance to the tune of a harmonious global village - so why can't the UN punish global polluters? If they were to forbid trade with countries that exceed certain levels of pollution, the world would certainly clean itself up in a hurry.

We have discussed a global fresh air bank in our previous books, looked at how some countries have contributed a lot to this cause while others contribute only pollution - which is unfair and very selfish. The UN should set guidelines for conservation starting at about 10% of every country's land to be dedicated as National Parks. There need be no fancy facilities or interpretive centers, just set aside large areas of the wild and keep them that way forever.

Trees clean the air and produce fresh oxygen (6 tons a year per hectare), and parks provide clean drinking water. If there isn't a lot of land readily available for Parks, Governments should buy vast tracts of land near existing parks and reclaim it by planting trees - nature will do the rest. Nature always flourishes when left alone.

Countries that can afford it, and countries that produce great amounts of pollution, should set aside 20% (or more) of their land for National Parks. The United States, for example, has vast areas of unproductive land in the west - semi-desert. Why not reforest the waste and have it produce oxygen? Australia should do the same with their central and western areas - bring in water by pipeline, irrigate the arid land and turn the desert into lush, green forest.

Efforts must be made to keep the Siberian boreal jungle undisturbed. It is too large and important to be tampered with. The loss of that forest would seriously or fatally damage the world's climate and ecology.

It is also very important that mountains be protected, mostly by National Parks. Mountains are weather makers, air purifiers and a source of most drinking water. If one pollutes a mountain river, one is like a bird that fouls its own nest - a very bad, stupid bird.

The entire American and Canadian Rockies should be protected with National Park status. So should the Pyrenees, the Alps, the Apennines, the Carpathians and the Balkan Ranges, where nature has been devastated and is very sick and nearly dead.

The opinion that industry and development destroys forestation is correct. However, in underdeveloped countries, poor people cut down trees on a daily basis, just to cook their meals. In some Asian and African countries, most of the forest is gone. What can be done? If the wealthier countries of the world want to help, they could create sources of solar, wind and hydro energy to replace wood burning and encourage the poorer countries to initiate reforestation.

We need a world with more big trees and fewer big stumps!

To quote from the wisdom and simple philosophy of our native peoples, "Take care of the land and it will take care of you. Take what you need from the land, but need what you take."

If modern man would live that native wisdom, we would not need National Parks and Wardens to guard them. The world would be green, healthy and beautiful. We should stop wasting the wonders of our natural world and display more respect and love for them. In the end, love can work miracles.

The Author

People, who speak out when they have strong opinions and stand for something, tend to be labeled "crusaders", and provoke extreme responses – we love them or hate them. The author definitely stands for the green, prisitine Rockies.

George Brybycin is a humble, frugal and totally non-materialist who has strongly defined goals in his life and realizes them step by step. He is a doer. His books feature Nature, especially the mountains and most particularly, his beloved Canadian Rockies. He also expresses strong opinions on a wide spectrum of subjects.

As our small, complex world is becoming more and more interwoven, George touches on global issues such as the world's ecology/environment, and is a staunch supporter of the National Parks concept. He is an artist and a passionate man but tries to be realistic in his pursuit of reason over passion.

George tries to convince the world that we must reclaim much of the devastated, wastelands we have created and bring them back to their original, natural state. He tries to show that if each of the world's countries will set aside 10 - 20% of their area for National Parks, then and only then, will the quality of our lives and the health of our world achieve a satisfactory level and ensure Earth's survival. If we continue to destroy our green areas at the present rate, there will soon be no way back.

Many call George one of the most prolific author/photographer in Canada and the fact that he has published 30 pictorial volumes speaks to his being the most prolific mountain photographer of them all.

George has chosen a very difficult, even dangerous field as his passion/profession. Exploring the remote wilderness; climbing high, challenging mountains; facing a variety of potentially dangerous animals and natural hazards - avalanches, blizzards, freezing temperatures, thunderstorms, icy rivers and so on.

These things are not the average family picnic. And, strange but true, George loves it all.

George has climbed 400 mountains to date and still continues the quest to do more. His books are sold at a very low price, often at cost, in order to make them available to as many people as possible. Thus he brings his green message to the world.

If you haven't guessed by now, green is George's favourite colour. He has planted over 2,000 trees to date in an effort to green up our increasingly gray world – and his last will goes to trees - thousands of them. George's green legacy.

George feels privileged, happy and grateful for the opportunity to live in the paradise of the Rocky Mountains - where the quality of life is as high as the mountains; where the air is fresh and full of inspiration; where beauty is in great abundance and where people try to live their lives on nature's terms.

Photographic studies by George Brybycin :

The High Rockies	Cosmopolitan Calgary
Colourful Calgary	Banff and Jasper N.P.
Our Fragile Wilderness	The Rockies: Wildlife
The Rocky Mountains	The Majestic Rockies
Banff National Park	Emerald Waters of the Rockies
Jasper National Park	The Canadian Rockies Panoramas
Colourful Calgary II	Eternal Rockies
Wildlife in the Rockies	Calgary, the Stampede City and Environs
Rocky Mountain Symphony	Alpine Meadows
Enchanted Wilderness	The Rockies, British Columbia, The North
Wilderness Odyssey	Rocky Mountain Odyssey
Rocky Mountain Symphony II	Banff & Jasper National Parks II
Romance of the Rockies	The Canadian Rockies
Calgary - The Sunshine City	The Canadian Rockies Panoromas II
The Living Rockies	The Pristine Rockies

Front cover: Golden autumn in the Rockies
Back cover: Lake Louise, Banff National Park.

This book was created and produced in Alberta.
Design: George Brybycin
Typeset: K & H United Co.
Printed in China by Everbest Printing Co.

Copyright © 2001 by GB Publishing
All rights reserved
No parts of this book may be reproduced in any form without written permission from the publisher, except for brief passages quoted by a reviewer.

ISBN 0-919029-31-0

For current list, please write to:
GB PUBLISHING, Box 6292, Station D,
Calgary, Alberta Canada T2P 2C9

Take a hike but ...
take only pictures,
leave only footprints,
this is the pristine wilderness,
fragile and very vulnerable.

George Brybycin's collection of 20,000 35mm colour slides is FOR SALE.
Subjects include: The Rockies, Western and Northern Canada, Calgary, The 1988 Olympics, Alaska, The Western U.S. and the World. Also available is the collection of all 30 George's books. Offers may be tendered to GB Publishing at the address above.